Commendations (
by Jim C

As a former acquisitions editor for a Christian publisher, I always approached new manuscripts with a solitary question: *'Does this work demand to be published?'* Few met the threshold. But every once in a long while, something would come along that knocked my socks off; something like Jim Graham's *"personalisations"* of Paul's rich epistles.

Every page draws me in as if I were a privileged eavesdropper thumbing through the devotional diary of a humble, passionate lover of God. *The God Life* is nothing short of a spiritual treasure! How fortunate we are that Jim overcame his initial reluctance to sharing these keen and intimate insights with the public.

George Otis, Jr
Chairman, The Sentinel Group and
Pioneer of the Transformations series of videos

The highest compliment that a teacher can pay another teacher is that of wanting to sit at his feet and glean as much as possible from him. Jim Graham's understanding of the letters of St. Paul brings the Scripture to life in a manner that deeply impacts the reader.

It has been my heartfelt privilege to be the recipient of Jim's profound insights into Scripture on several occasions – both when speaking at International conferences with Ellel Ministries and, on a one-to-one basis, when I sought him out for his deep insights on complex issues. Jim has been for me a true *"father in the faith"*, whose life and testimony bore the fruit of a person who knew and experienced the intimate counsel of the Lord Himself.

I recall one occasion when I needed his counsel over a matter that deeply distressed me and with complete seriousness, but also with a quiet hint of his Scottish wit, he looked at me and said *"Alistair – we must learn*

always to out-live rather than out-argue – and then the Lord will do the rest".
That one statement has stayed with me for years and deeply impacted me
then – as it still does today.

The God-Life will be one of my personal study and teaching resources.
It has been written by a man who has, himself, lived life in a manner that
reflects the Kingdom of God, with integrity and humility.

Rev. Dr. Alistair P. Petrie
Executive Director, Partnership Ministries
www.partnershipministries.org

When the Lord called me from the pastorate of Gold Hill Baptist Church
in Buckinghamshire, to another in Surrey, Jim Graham was appointed as
my successor. This gentle and gracious Scotsman drew respect and made
lasting friendships easily. He was a convinced charismatic, evangelical
believer like myself, so there was no theological hiccup. I was there for
seven years. Jim stayed for the rest of his life.

Now, as he prepares for his next engagement (in glory), Jim has
released his final gift to the body of Christ – his own version of most of
Paul's letters. It is a fitting climax to his unique ministry. It is the legacy of
someone who has loved and lived these scriptures.

The editor's description, in the subtitle of the book, could not be more
apt: for it certainly is a *personalised version*. Paul's concerns, his conflicts and
his compassion come across vividly. The original readers are more real. And
contemporary readers could feel they had received a love letter from God.

It is, of course, a paraphrase rather than a word for word translation,
so the saintly character of this translator can be discerned. Those who have
known Jim will value even more this superb interpretation.

Rev J. David Pawson
*Internationally renowned Bible teacher and
former Pastor of Gold Hill Baptist Church*

When I read Jim Graham's interpretation of Paul's letters I hear the voice of a man I have come to know and love very deeply. When I read them as his pastor, I hear the depth of his understanding of God and of faith reverberate across every word. When I read them as the pastor of the church he once led, I sense the voice of a brilliant pastor.

Jim's interpretation of Paul's words plants them deeply in my soul. I sense the tenderness of truth matched with the grit of grace. Jim has not only brought Paul's words to life, he has unveiled some of Paul's thinking. As I read Jim's paraphrase, I was caught up in the sheer power of the word of God and its ability to cut through the mediocrity of much of modernity and get to the heart of the matter.

Rev Malcolm Duncan

Pastor, Gold Hill Baptist Church

What a remarkable treasure has been unearthed in this publishing of Jim's reflective "translation" of some of Paul's letters. Throughout my journey as a follower of Jesus Christ I have longed for contact with true elders in the Body of Christ, those who would demonstrate authentic Christianity and speak genuine wisdom. I have found this in Jim Graham, and now I'm overjoyed to have access to this unexpected resource of Jim's inspired pondering on the letters of Paul. This book will provide, for generations to come, a remarkable insight into the thoughts and words of Paul, as he mentored the early church. Thank you so much Jim for all you have imparted into the Body of Christ and, not least this extraordinary book.

David Cross

Regional Director of Western Europe
for Ellel Ministries International

The God life is a remarkable book by an extraordinary man of God. Jim Graham says because men and women have chosen to give up God, He has taken his brake off society and this teaching shows us how to welcome him back.

Jim is a Holy Spirit anointed and gifted writer. His inspirational insights into the epistles are profound. He weaves his way through Paul's writings with thought provoking depth and understanding. It is almost like God himself was dictating this work to Jim!

I unreservedly recommend this book, whatever you have on your reading list don't miss this!

Jill Southern-Jones
Regional Director of East Asia for Ellel Ministries
International and former
Director of Ellel Ministries Pierrepont

Jim Graham, in giving us this brilliant paraphrase of the Pauline Epistles, has walked in the steps of J.B Philips, Ken Taylor and Eugene Peterson, all of whom gave us great paraphrases. As I read the text I knew in my heart that God would use this great book to take people deeper into God's Holy Word.

George Verwer
Founder of Operation Mobilisation

Publisher's Note

Jim Graham has been one of my closest and most precious friends for almost twenty-five years. He has taught at different Ellel Centres and Conferences on many occasions and His fatherly input, encouragement, correction and direction have always been immensely valued.

I knew Jim wasn't well at the beginning of 2016 as he had cancelled some teaching appointments, because of what he thought must be flu. But on the 19th March 2016 I received an email from him, containing the detailed diagnosis of his condition by his medical consultants. In this he said: *"In reality, Peter, it looks like I am heading to the finishing line. I am content and completely free of anxiety. Please pray that I will finish well! Looks like, too, Peter that my teaching days are over."*

My eyes filled with tears as I dwelt on those many years of rich fellowship and the prospect of Jim no longer being part of God's family on earth. I will never forget the few hours we were privileged to spend together on the 6th April, mainly talking about the Lord, and the precious days Jim was now living through, with his family around him, awaiting his call home.

It was not until the 25th April that I heard, via our leaders in Northern Ireland, of the existence of Jim's personal *'translations'* of Paul's Epistles. I wrote to him immediately, urging him to consider allowing them to be published. Very graciously, he arranged for a copy of all the letters he had completed to be sent to me, together with a Preface he had just written, should the material ever be published.

Prior to the establishment of Ellel Ministries in 1986, I was a professional publisher with a series of companies. Three times in those fifteen exciting years in the trade, I was fortunate enough to discover and publish significant books and have the privilege of bringing them to the market as best-sellers. Moments like those are never forgotten.

But when I started to read *The God-Life*, I realized I was holding in my hand something far more precious and valuable than anything I had ever discovered in the secular world. This was a 'publishing moment' to exceed all others. For when I read the text of *The God-Life*, I realized I was not only reading a manuscript of outstanding significance and quality, but it was as if I was standing on holy ground!

From time to time I had heard Jim illustrate his teaching with profoundly impacting readings, but I had no idea that they were extracts from his personalized translations of most of Paul's Epistles. In his email Jim had said *"my teaching days are over"*. But what I was reading was so profound that I sensed the very opposite would be the case – Jim's wider teaching ministry to the whole Body of Christ was only just beginning!

Paul wrote many of his letters in prison to teach and encourage the saints in the developing new churches. He had no idea that his writings would form part of the New Testament and be available to teach and encourage the saints for the rest of time. And in a similar way, when Jim wrote these personalized translations of Paul's letters he was doing it in obedience to a personal Word from the Lord, but largely, as he thought, for his own benefit. But now the whole Church, until Jesus comes again, can benefit from Jim Graham's profound, Holy Spirit inspired, understanding of Paul's amazing letters.

The book may be unfinished, in that Jim's final illness prevented him from completing all of Paul's letters. But don't let that prevent you from treasuring every page of this precious gift from one of God's choice saints to God's people everywhere.

It has been an incredible privilege to prepare *The God-Life* for publication and my prayer is that these pages will enable Jim Graham's extraordinary teaching gift to be an inspirational blessing to countless other people, as they journey through life to their own finishing line.

Peter Horrobin
Founder of Ellel Ministries International
and Chairman of Sovereign World Ltd.

The God-Life

Romans • Galatians • Ephesians • Philippians • Colossians
1 Thessalonians • 2 Thessalonians • 1 Timothy

The God-Life

Letters of the Apostle Paul

as personalised by

Jim Graham

Sovereign World

Published by Sovereign World Ltd
PO Box 784
Ellel
Lancaster
LA1 9DA
United Kingdom

www.sovereignworld.com
Twitter: @sovereignworld
Facebook: www.facebook.com/sovereignworld

Published June 2016

ISBN: 978-1-85240-744-5

British Library Cataloguing-in-Publication Data
A catalogue record for this book is available from the British Library.

Typesetting and cover design by www.zaccmedia.com

Cover picture by artist Lars Justinen licensed and reproduced by permission from www.goodsalt.com

Contents

Foreword

By Rev Malcolm Duncan

ONE OF THE GREATEST DANGERS facing today's Church is a lack of understanding of the Scriptures. In the words of Amos 8:11, it feels like we are living in a land of famine. We hunger for the truth of God's Holy Word.

I do not suggest that such a lack is universal, but where it exists the results are plain to see – apathy in believers, prayerlessness, a weakening of our understanding of the Gospel and a failure to engage confidently with our culture. Worst of all, perhaps, this lack results in the sufferers forgetting what God is like, and when we forget what He is like we also lose sight of who we are.

So how does one address such a lack? By encouraging people to read the Bible, to remember its centrality and to allow the truth of God's word to penetrate our hearts, our imaginations and our lives once again. By allowing the Holy Spirit to enliven the word of God to us and in us, we become people who find life in God's word because God's life is active and formative in us. As we allow the Word of God to seep into our souls, the presence of God seeps out of our lives. The equation is really very simple, what is in us shows through us. There has never been a more urgent need to return to the truth of God's word and let it saturate our lives. The future shape of the Church depends upon it. We need to discover the God-life.

Jim Graham's work in these interpretations of Paul offers us the chance to re-discover some of the implications of the Apostle's words. Jim captures not only the meaning, but the sentiment, heart, passion and character of Paul. It is no wonder that he does so – Jim has been studying, reading and preaching from Paul's letters for almost seventy years. Jim's work in *The God-Life* has a powerful resonance with those of us who long to see the Bible come alive in the hearts of believers and in the Church.

Jim used a phrase through much of his preaching that I am reminded of. He would often hold the Bible in his hand and tap it with the other hand and say to those who were listening, *'I didn't write this stuff!'* His point was clear, if we are offended, challenged or upset by the words of Scripture we must take those issues up with the author, not with the messenger. In *The God-Life* Jim gives us his own unique understanding of Paul, but as he does so I think He is bringing Paul to us in a new, fresh, accessible and deeply challenging way. Yet Jim's understanding of Paul's letters offers us life, hope and a new depth of understanding.

I have three great privileges when it comes to Jim Graham. The first, and to me the most important, is that we are close friends. Put simply, we love one another. The second is that I am his pastor. It has been a deep joy to walk with Anne and him. The third is that I have the joy of leading Gold Hill, the church he led for almost thirty years. We share a love for the church and its people both here and everywhere where God's people are. We also share a commitment to God's word and an openness to the Holy Spirit. All of these strands combine into the tapestry of his interpretation of Paul's words – a tapestry which has been slowly formed in Jim over these past ten years of reflection, prayer and ministry. These words have been given time to mature and to form properly. They are rich and they are deep.

When I read his interpretation of Paul's letters I hear the voice of a man I have come to know and love very deeply. When I read them as his pastor, I hear the depth of his understanding of God and of faith reverberate across every word. When I read them as the pastor of the church he once led, I sense the voice of a brilliant pastor.

Jim's interpretation of Paul's words plants them deeply in my soul. I sense the tenderness of truth matched with the grit of grace. Jim has not only brought Paul's words to life, he has unveiled some of Paul's thinking. As I read Jim's paraphrase, I was caught up in the sheer power of the word of God and its ability to cut through the mediocrity of much of modernity and get to the heart of the matter.

Apart from Jim's deep love of his family and his own amazing integrity and love, the three great attributes of his life have been his love of God's word, his openness to God's Spirit and his commitment to God's church. Each of these three strands can be heard in Jim's take on Paul's letters. Like J.B. Philips and Eugene Peterson before him, Jim has dug into the text of Paul. He has wrestled through the challenges to get to the sentiment of the great apostle. Jim has unveiled something of the passion, love and determination of Paul for those he wrote to and in so doing he has brought the text to life again, for those who have ears to hear and hearts willing to listen to what God might say to us again today.

Rev. Malcolm Duncan
Pastor, Gold Hill Baptist Church
Chalfont St. Peter, UK

Foreword

By Rev Stuart McAlpine

Paul's description of the leaders of the Jerusalem Church (Peter, James and John) can be applied to the life-long pastoral and apostolic ministry of Jim Graham. He is an *"esteemed pillar"* (Galatians 2:9). The influence of his wisdom and teaching, of his spiritual ministrations, of the example of his life, of his personal sanctity and intimacy with God, has seeped, soaked and spread throughout the church, affecting tens of thousands of lives, multiple ministry and mission agencies, nations and generations. Why? Because he was a man who walked humbly with his God and hung on His every Word.

I first learned of Pastor Graham through my father, Campbell McAlpine, who had such love and deep respect for him, and they ministered together on countless occasions, especially at Gold Hill Baptist Church. Little did I know that a time would come when I would have the privilege of sharing a ministry assignment with him at an Ellel Ministries' Conference, and get first-hand experience of that same gravitational pull of Father, Son and Holy Spirit, that exuded from his preaching and his personhood.

In characteristically modest fashion, Jim Graham said that he was *"very hesitant"* to allow this remarkable text to be published, and then it was with *"great reluctance"* that he eventually conceded. Such is his love and honor of the Word that he demurred at the thought that it would be treated as a 'translation'. We should lift the burden of that word 'translation' from his shoulders and from this godly enterprise, and try to capture exactly what he has succeeded in doing in this presentation of the Epistles.

It may help to say what it is not. It is not a 'translation', in the sense that the meaning of every word of the original text has been literally rendered into another language. It is not merely a paraphrase, nor is it trying to be self-consciously vernacular. It is not that '*The God Life*' does not have any of these nuances, it is just that it is not exclusively marked by them. Mind you, it should be read as widely as any such renderings. Although not a literal translation from Greek to English, it is faithful to the original and captures and expresses its resonance and richness. Although it is not a consciously informal attempt to provide a contemporary-style communication, it does speak in readily understandable terms. This is in a category all of its own. So what is it?

When I started to read '*The God-Life*', and allow the Holy Spirit to speak to me through it, three words came to my mind in quick succession that captured for me the essence of what I was encountering as a reader.

- The first word was '**transposition**', which is the action of taking something and presenting it in a new way – in this case, a way that can be comprehensible and communicable to the reader.

Charles Haddon Spurgeon spoke of the need to study the Bible until our blood became "*bibline*". Jim Graham has embedded himself in the text, and it is in his blood. He has succeeded in imagining the original context of the readers, identifying with the heart and mind of Paul, the writer, and interpreting the meaning of the message.

Somehow, he has managed to transpose all of that into an integrated expression in which all the non-negotiable elements of Bible study (observation, interpretation and application) are present. No Bible Study leader should be without it!

We do not feel that we are on the outside of the text, wondering which key on our hermeneutical chain is going to fit the lock and let us in.

On the contrary, the text is unwrapped and opened up, in a way that invites us to receive its gifts of exhortation and instruction, with a sense of immediacy, as if we, the readers, are the Ephesians, the Galatians, the Thessalonians that are listening to it for the first time. There is no Bible Study of the Epistles that would not be enlivened and enriched by a reading of this transposition.

- The second word was '**transmission**'. If something is transmitted, it gets through from one person to another. It is one thing to transpose something, but another to do it in a way that it has a voice that speaks its truth into the life of the reader. Jim's godly expression of the text becomes an experience, as the truth and power of that text addresses and adheres to the spirit of the reader.

There is Paul's voice, clearly up-close and personal. There is Jim's voice, clearly pastoral, as the words of scripture are inseparable from the words he has transcribed. But above all, there is the voice of the Paraclete, the Holy Spirit, the author and interpreter of the Word, transmitting its appeal to our hearts. Whoever has ears to hear let them tune in, listen and hear this transmission.

- The third word is '**transformation.**' The last sentence of Pastor Graham's Preface reminds us that the reality of Scripture impacts our lives in a *"deeply transforming way."* The outcome from reading this script will not be challenge but change. Yes, you will be informed, but if you allow the Holy Spirit to do what He does best, and reveal the will and word of God to you as you read, and relate it to every nook and cranny of your life, then you will no longer be conformed to the patterns of the world but transformed by the renewing of your mind.

There will be thousands who will be so grateful to Pastor Graham for allowing us to read the Epistles with him, and learn from his example of how to interleave our lives with the pages of Scripture. Yes, we are reading the Epistles, but in a very poignant sense, we are also reading the personal devotions, meditations and spiritual journalings of a man who cannot get enough of the voice of God as it speaks through His Word.

With humility, Jim Graham quietly admits that this is *"one of the best things I have ever done for my own personal growth and development."* Second to the complete text of your Bible, this may be *"one of the best things"* that you have read in a long, long time for your *"own personal growth and development."* How I pray that this is so, and that *'The God-Life'* becomes a *'God-send'*.

Rev Stuart McAlpine
Pastor, Church of Christ our Shepherd
Capitol Hill, Washington DC. USA

Author's Preface

IT WAS A WARM, BALMY, SUNNY afternoon in South Portugal. Anne hadn't been feeling well and was resting, and I was sitting enjoying the view of the lovely garden outside the villa, when I sensed God was speaking to me (I don't hear voices!). I think He was saying that He wanted me to 'translate' the New Testament. I wasn't quite sure what that meant but I immediately got up, got in the car, and drove down to the little village of Corvoiero. I bought three exercise books and returned to the villa.

The only Bible I had with me was a slim NIV New Testament. I turned to Paul's Letter to the Ephesians and the first Chapter and I began to write. Incredibly, my writing began to flow easily. For most of my life I have had the amazing opportunity to reflect on Scripture and I found that the reflections of the years came clearly into my mind.

I had always tried to 'imagine' the context in which the text was set; where was Paul when he was writing this? How was he feeling – lonely, frustrated, elated, anxious, grateful, compassionate, concerned? Who did he have in mind when he was writing – a local church; a group of churches; an individual? What was the main thing that he wanted to communicate – was it theological, practical, personal, relational? Was he writing to encourage, inform, correct?

All of these things occupied my mind and I began to enjoy these reflections as I wrote. I am not a Greek scholar but I have a fair understanding of New Testament Greek and I have always been determined to get to grips with the original text and handle it with integrity. I have found that there is a richness in the Greek language that sometimes is absent from an English translation. I have always tried to communicate this – hopefully in an unpretentious way! All of this – and probably much more – lies behind these 'translations'.

Above everything else I am deeply concerned that I would never infringe the authority of Scripture. To call these writings I have done 'translations' could so easily do this and for this reason I have been very hesitant to allow them to be published. I hold the authority of Scripture very highly and see the Old as well as the New Testament to be the inspired, authoritative, unquestioned Word of God.

Over these past years when I have continued to 'unpack' these pieces of Scripture I have come to realise that this is perhaps one of the best things I have ever done for my own personal spiritual growth and development. It has been such a delight and privilege for me in the midst of a busy schedule of preaching, teaching, and lecturing to 'sneak' an hour or so alone with my Bible open, without any intrusion of Commentary or other help, and try to 'hear' what the text is actually saying into my life. I have constantly been staggered by the relevance for me of what is written there.

Over these years, when I have dared and ventured (while I have been preaching or teaching in public) to read from these 'translations', I have always had someone ask what I was reading from. In spite of my great reluctance to allow these to be published I have been encouraged during these final days of my life to do so. Please receive them, in all their humanity and inadequacy, for what they are – the thrilling reality of Holy Scripture impacting an ordinary man's life in a deeply transforming way.

Jim Graham
April 2016

THE GOD-LIFE AND ITS FOUNDATIONS

Paul's Letter to the

Romans

Paul's Letter to the

ROMANS

Y OU DO NOT KNOW ME, for we have had no contact with each other and we live 1500 miles apart so I want to introduce myself to you. My name is Paul and my credentials for writing to you are first of all that my life has been surrendered to and is constantly submitted to the desires of the One whom God promised to send into our world as His Anointed One. He came out of eternity into history with a human name, a name which means He will save people from the condemnation and consequences of sin.

Secondly, I have an absolute conviction, dramatically born in a completely unforgettable and an entirely unexpected Christ-resurrected encounter on the road to Damascus, that God has chosen and called me to carry the transforming Name of Jesus Christ to those who are not Jews. This conviction has been supernaturally and courageously affirmed by a God-sent man called Ananias who was unknown to me.

Thirdly, I have been left in no doubt whatsoever that my life is no longer my own to control and direct as I wish but is entirely and radically devoted to the life-transforming, religion-destroying, and hope-inspiring

Good News of God. I was blinded not only physically on the Damascus Road but I realised, at that time, I had been blinded spiritually throughout my life.

Until that point I did not recognise that this Good News in Jesus had long-since been at the heart of the message so powerfully declared and carried by God's chosen servants in the precious Old Testament, which had been such a fundamental part of my life since I was a child. Clearly, when this same Jesus became flesh of our flesh and bone of our bone in His miraculous birth in Bethlehem, He was a descendent of our great king and recognised prophet, David, who lived a thousand years earlier.

He was exposed to the same rigours of temptation as we are and yet His submission and dependence on the Holy Spirit enabled Him to remain absolutely pure and magnificently sinless. His defeat of death, hell, and the grave conclusively and dynamically demonstrated Him not only to be the Son of man but also the Son of God. He is the One who came out of heaven into earth to redeem mankind and reign in His Kingdom.

It is from Him and for Him that I have received this completely unearned and undeserved privilege and responsibility to issue this invitation to those who are not Jews to enter the Kingdom of God under the lordship of His Son, Jesus, by trusting in who Jesus is and in what He has done. It is for this reason that I am writing to you that you would know that you are included in the family of God.

This letter is addressed to all those who live in the great city of Rome who are cherished by God and set free to live lives that are markedly different from those around you because of Him. May the sheer, undeserved generosity and limitless wholeness and well-being that comes from God, our Father, and His Son, Jesus, who is both Lord and Messiah, rest upon you.

Right at the beginning I want you to know that though we have never met, my heart is overflowing with gratitude to God for all that I hear right across the nations of your remarkable obedience to the revealed will of

God. This, obviously, is the impact of your Community of Faith because of what Jesus Christ has done for you individually and now corporately and congregationally.

No one else can authenticate this apart from God to whom I give my absolute allegiance. I have demonstrated this allegiance by my now fearless and forthright declaration of the Good News about who Jesus is and why He came into the world. He certainly knows how constantly and consistently I intercede for you all. I am asking Him at this very time to make it possible for me to be with you in person, someday soon, so that I may share my love and encouragement with you.

You see, God has so overwhelmed me with His sheer, undeserved and certainly unearned favour, heaping wonder upon wonder upon me, that I want so desperately to share with you some of His unbelievable and astounding blessings, to affirm and strengthen you even more than you already are.

Be assured it will certainly not be one-way traffic for I have a great hunger in my heart to receive some of what God has given you that we may go on together to honour and serve Him more effectively. You need to know that for a long time my heart and spirit have been focused on you, because Rome is so strategic for the fulfilling of God's purposes throughout the world. You have been on my schedule regularly but, so far, it hasn't worked out for me to travel to you. It has pleased God to use me in so many places among non-Jews and I long that some of that richness, assurance, and security could be imparted to you.

I am deeply committed to all men everywhere regardless of the cultural, social, racial or religious backgrounds they may have. I honour those who are intellectually sharp and astute as well as those who find ideas and concepts hard to grasp. It is for this reason my enthusiasm knows no bounds when I think about the possibility of coming to you there in Rome and sharing the amazing and astounding Good News that God has given us in His Son, Jesus.

What I once dismissed so arrogantly I now embrace eagerly, regardless of what people may say or think of me. This Good News from God has the incredible ability to change lives, revolutionize character, and inspire hope in all who will receive it, believe it, and live it; this applies to Jews first of all as God's chosen people and then for non-Jews.

You see, in this Good News a holy covering and cleansing from God is imparted to sinful humanity not by us trying harder but by us trusting more in what He has so gloriously and perfectly done in His Son, Jesus, on our behalf. I have no idea why it took me so long to realise what the prophet Habakkuk was saying when he declared that works are always tied to faith but faith is never tied to works – salvation can never be earned BY our hands but it must always be expressed THROUGH our hands.

Because of the context in which you are living – the overpowering confines of the Roman Empire – right at the beginning of this letter, I need to share some serious and disturbing things with you about the Good News of God's anger. Let's get two things clear about this – one, God's anger is not because he is irascible, petulant, or bad-tempered (these things characterize human anger!) and two, God's anger is not simply a principle built into the moral order of the universe. God's anger is a deeply personal reaction.

This ensures that God is not indifferent and disinterested in what is going on in His world but He is constantly involved. His anger is the reaction of a holy God, who makes good things, to sinful people who spoil these good things causing misery and heart-ache for themselves and for others. His anger is part of the revelation of God to man – from eternity into history.

God's anger is evoked by ungodliness – where men and women ignore Him; disregard Him; discard Him and live as if He did not exist. Inevitably that leads to unrighteousness because our relationship with God and our regard for Him – or lack of it – will always affect our relationships with people and respect for them. Idolatry will always lead to immorality.

Because men and women have chosen to give God up, God has taken His brake off society. Godlessness will always be accompanied by wickedness in some form or another. We need to be aware that God substantially and consistently is a God of revelation. Since the morning of time and amongst all people everywhere, God has put creation around us and conscience within us. The created world around us speaks of His power and the moral law within us speaks of His character; consequently, the atheist and the agnostic are left without a leg to stand on. The one thing that can never be done before God is to plead ignorance and innocence.

All men everywhere and at all times have known God but they have stifled and suppressed the truth and deliberately dishonoured and disregarded Him. God is angry because in the minds of men what they thought was cleverness was, in fact, confusion and in the instincts of men what they thought was fulfilment was, in fact, futility. They traded revelation for reason and constructed their own ideas of God and consequently believed a lie rather than the truth about Him. So man's tradition took over from God's truth and he made God in his own image. Inevitably, man's imagination was quickly followed by man's invention and his worship became centred on what he had created rather than on the Creator.

The dire consequence of this is that God said, "If that's the way you want it, then that's the way you can have it!" Please understand that God doesn't make man sin but He does let man sin. When man gives God up then man inescapably goes into idolatry. When God gives man over to what he wants to do then man inescapably goes into immorality.

Immorality is not the cause of God's anger; it is the consequence of His anger. Foundational to God's creation is the relationship between male and female with all its enormously satisfying potential for cooperation rather than competition. Inherent in that relationship is a strong, powerful, driving sexuality.

When God's railings around human sexuality are removed, it expresses itself in lust rather than love and in perversion rather than purity. Let's go over the ground again – this happens when man chooses to disregard, dismiss, and discard God and substitutes his own reason for God's revelation and expresses that in worshipping material objects rather than spiritual reality. So the human takes the place of the divine and religion takes the place of reality.

Let me say it again, God does not give us up, but He does give us over to what we want to do and says, "If that's the way you want it, then that's the way you can have it!". The result is that unrestrained perversion issued in lesbianism and homosexuality – and an awesome blight spread throughout the world.

In addition to all of that, because men and women regarded it as irrelevant and paltry to hold on to all that God had said and shown, God allowed them to have their own way and to think in ways that even the animal kingdom did not come close to and to behave in a base and degrading manner.

You see, alarmingly, when you dispense with God in your life not only does He allow you to think what you like, but He allows you to do what you want. Society, not just superficially, but fundamentally, develops a liking for doing all kinds of wrong things; dragging others down with it; being deeply discontented with what it has and constantly demanding more and more; and so behaving in a dehumanized way. It becomes consumed with what others have and thinks of them in a warped and twisted way enamoured with a celebrity culture; eliminates others in thought and word as well as physically becoming obsessed with self; wanting always to cause trouble and destroy peace; uses underhand methods to put itself in a good light; and puts the worst construction and interpretation on things, giving a distorted picture of what is actually true.

It whispers about others behind their backs; speaks openly about others to destroy their reputation and good name; thinks and speaks of God with bitterness because He puts the brakes on so limiting their freedom to do whatever takes their fancy; regards those in authority with defiance and rudeness; puts on a veneer and pretends to be, to have, and to do what it isn't, hasn't, and can't.

7

As if all these things were not enough godless society persistently thinks of more ways to do wrong; ignores the wisdom, experience, and advice of those who have walked the road before it and considers them completely out-of-touch with the reality of the hour. It revels in blurring the distinction between right and wrong and despises absolutes. It becomes unreliable and undependable so that promises made are broken and responsibility accepted is forgotten.

It is insensitive to the needs of others and compassion is replaced with selfishness and even cruelty. Human society is inconsistent in that it does wrong itself, but condemns these same wrongs in others. And yet, astonishingly, irrationally and confusingly, human society is insurrectionist in that it not only does wrong itself but approves, affirms, and encourages others to do, think, and say these very wrong things.

Just as from time to time there is a taste of heaven on earth when God breaks in to fulfil His own sovereign purposes, so here you have a taste of hell on earth because God has left people to do what they want. What I have written to you is not an unhealthy obsession with stern moralising, but, as I said earlier, I am discussing the context of the Roman Empire which is the context in which you are living. Be assured, however, that it will forever be like that when a society dismisses and ignores God!

∼CHAPTER 2 ∼

But I need to move now from the general situation of the humanistic secularism of the pagan-obsessed, idolatry-crazed, Jehovah-despising Roman Empire to say something which is much more individual and personal. I also want to move from what is happening now in the present – (and you, of all people, are so overwhelmingly aware of it) – to what will happen in the future – a Day when God will finally and fully reveal His anger as never before. If God is a good God then He must make all things right – justice and righteousness demand that!

There are three questions that must be asked and answered – WHO will God judge? WHAT will God judge? And HOW will God judge? The first question is 'Who will stand in the dock?' Those of you who condemn sin in others yet are guilty of these very same things yourselves will be condemned by their own track record – your liking for the wrong things: your discontented grumbling with your lot; your putting the worst construction on things and painting a worse picture than is actually true; your whispering unkind, unhelpful, destructive things about people behind their backs; your pretending to be, to have, and to do what you aren't, haven't, and can't; your making promises that you cannot keep; and so on.

You do these things not in ignorance of God's judgment, but in awareness of it. You pass judgment on others although you are restricted by the limitations of your humanity and your own lives bear witness to the same destructive, self-righteous stuff. Do you imagine God will turn a blind eye to that so far as you are concerned? You are blind, delusional, and living in a fantasy world if you trade on the idea that God would not hurt a fly; will accept any kind of behaviour; and because He does not send His bills in every month He will never do so. God, in His overwhelming and undeserved generosity is giving you time to recognise and face up to what is really in your own heart and life and get it dealt with by Him and begin living in a new and godly way before others.

Be assured God will judge habitual and hypocritical sinners who condone sin by allowing others to live, unchecked, in an ungodly way and who condemn sins in others that they clearly practice themselves. Don't trade on the fact that God's judgment doesn't fall on you now, but rather identify behaviour which is unacceptable to God; articulate it precisely before Him; choose unreservedly and wholeheartedly to abandon that particular way of behaving and live differently from now on.

The second question I want to address is: 'What will God judge?' Be assured God will judge the things we say and do and the lives that we live. The big issue here is, 'How much good do I need to do in order to be counted as one who does good?' The clear answer is, 'The one who does good all the time, continuously, without ever faltering, and with all of his or her personality'. If you are going to be judged on the good deeds that you do, then the pass-mark is one hundred per cent. Righteousness is like a chain – break one link and you break the whole chain.

I am trying so hard to get you through being captured by self-righteousness and hypocrisy because there is literally no one – apart from Jesus Christ – who can say, 'I have lived a perfect life forever without blemish or fault!' Please notice that with regard to those who are focused on and obsessed by themselves; who have deliberately chosen to ignore the Good News of God's undeserved favour towards them and have pursued godlessness; there is no suggestion that they have to live that way continually and habitually. To stray into these paths just once, is sufficient to 'break the chain'.

God divides people into two groups; those who have done good in thought, word, and deed without ever or in any way faltering all their lives and those who have done evil just once. Each one of us will be in one of these two groups when the awesome displeasure of God falls. Religion will not protect or save anyone any more than paganism will. God is no respecter of persons.

Those who have never been involved in or influenced by Judaism who disregard God in their behaviour will be held accountable because they have unmistakeably seen God in the created world around them and have sensed God in the moral law within them. Their destiny is bleak uselessness. By the same token, those who have failed to keep the Commandments they were given by God face the condemnation of the tribunal of God because they did not keep every one of them without exception and in every way.

So far as God is concerned it is not our understanding that is the touchstone of judgment but our response in obedience to what we understand to be true. (The fact of the matter is that non-Jews, even though they may instinctively respect and respond to what God expects and demands from Jews, are not exempt from God's judgment because deep within their humanity they acknowledge the character and requirements of God, because of the fabric of the created world around them). The Day will come when all that up-till-now has been hidden will be laid bare before the Judge Himself. I have consistently declared this Good News that God has no favourites! Neither religious activities nor pagan practices will cover what has been hidden until then.

Let me address those who claim to be Jews – be very careful about where your confidence lies. You are so prone to feel superior because of the rules and regulations of your religion and the fact that God chose you in history for His special purposes. Undoubtedly God revealed His purposes to you and commanded you to a life-style that He prescribed. Because of this you patronise those who cannot see the way ahead; those who wander aimlessly without purpose or direction in their living. You set yourselves up as experts before those who do not even know the right questions to ask, far less giving the right answers. You boast of your maturity among the immature and your experience before the inexperienced. All of this simply because of your relationship to God and His revelation to you.

Surely you are a very favoured people. But here is the catastrophic tragedy – you want to impose truth on those around you but fail to embrace and express that same truth yourselves in the way you live. Let me ask you a number of searching and intrusive questions. You are opposed to taking from others what doesn't belong to you; but do you never get involved in that yourselves, as you rob people not only of money for religious purposes but of hope, legitimacy and dignity? You are very strong in condemning sexual immorality but infidelity and impurity are not unknown to you, are they?

You have a deep abhorrence against those who worship relying on material images created by their own hands and forging mental concepts that bear no resemblance whatsoever to the one and only true God who really is. Is it not true, however, that your own worship is empty, formal, unimpressive and completely unacceptable to God? You are so proud and arrogant that God has given you His Law but who is there among you who can claim they have obeyed that Law in every aspect and detail? Surely you know from the thunder-toned pronouncements of your prophets that God has been given a bad name among non-Jews because of your attitudes and activities.

You point to a visible, surgical procedure on the body of every male Jew as evidence that you are special and belong to God, but that is only valid when you demonstrate your surrender and submission to God by your obedience to what He has shown you. Be in no doubt whatsoever that disobedience invalidates what you claim to be unmistakeable evidence.

Do you not realise that non-Jews who live in such a way that they demonstrate God's moral law as part of the expression of their humanity, without being instructed as you have been (and without bearing that same physical evidence on their bodies) would be as likely to be accepted by God as you are? Those whom you despise and reject as unclean and unacceptable will rise up against you as evidence for the prosecution on Judgment Day in spite of all the ways God has blessed you and revealed Himself to you.

Jewishness is not about rules and regulations which are acknowledged and performed without any change of heart. Jewishness is about openness to God in soul and spirit so that God gets the honour and the glory and not you.

∼ CHAPTER 3 ∼

In the light of all that I have said, you who are Jews, reading this or listening to it being read, may well be asking, 'Is there no advantage at all in being born into a Jewish family and raised in the wonderful Covenants; the distinctive culture; and the clear commandments that give unmistakeable evidence of our God-favoured race?'

Let me disabuse you of that negative reaction and that disillusioning question. As Jews you have been unbelievably privileged and inexpressibly blessed in a multitude of ways. For example, your whole history bears indisputable testimony to the fact that we not only have a God who has ears, but our God has lips too – He speaks as well as listens!! He has never been guilty of hiding Himself from us but eagerly, enthusiastically, and with integrity He has consistently wanted to reveal Himself to us. You have had the responsibility of declaring to the whole of creation with clarity and authority, "This is what God says!".

The fact that some did not and have not lived their lives in the assurance and demonstration of this incredible reality does not and cannot make it null and void. God's character remains unimpaired and flawless. Your great ancestor, King David, said long ago, "God does what He says, and the verdicts that He gives are irreproachable." We leave ourselves totally exposed when we come to recognise the truth, that the flawless perfection and purity of God highlights our own glaring failures and blatant imperfections.

In the long run, what are you expecting God to do – turn a blind eye to all that is wrong and rotten in our humanity and allow it to continue without dealing with it rigorously? (I do realise that I am using human logic and human words to express and explain something which is far too big for me to convey to you!). It is quite inconceivable that God, being God, would behave in such a way to all that He has created. I have heard people say in the light of all of this – 'If my weakness shows His strength more clearly; and my failures affirm His faithfulness more firmly; and my humanity declares and demonstrates His divinity more convincingly; why would God judge me so severely?'

Be very careful when you are tempted to think in this way. It really is warped and twisted thinking! It ends up by saying, 'My ungodly and unprincipled behaviour is an excellent thing since it gives God a chance to show how good He is. Surely you cannot condemn a man for giving God a chance to show His justice?' Believe it or not we have actually been accused of preaching and teaching this contemptuous and intolerable stuff. To state it, as I have done, is to make it abundantly clear that the wrath of God's judgment is not misplaced.

Where does all this leave us? It is not a question of worse or better. I have made it abundantly clear that race or religion (or lack of it for that matter!) count for nothing because everyone, without exception, stands guilty before God.

You Jews should know this better than anyone else because a thousand years ago, in your Book of Praise, the writer of some of the Psalms found there declared more than once and in no uncertain terms that not a single, solitary soul on the face of the earth has a right relationship with God. There are no exceptions – everyone has a flawed understanding of God and every human effort to find Him as He really is futile and doomed to failure. This is an absolutely awesome fact and there is nothing casual about this for everyone has deliberately gone in the wrong direction and become soiled goods as a result. For all of us our best efforts do not cut it.

The way we speak causes death rather than life and our words can never be fully trusted. What we say not only wounds but causes paralysis rather than bringing freedom. Instead of speaking blessing over people, we do the opposite and bring confusion and heart-break. Wherever we go we cause injustice and bring disintegration and destruction into people's lives, leaving them broken and in despair. Far from bringing contentment and a sense of well-being into the human situation, we do the reverse of that. Worst of all, God is not taken seriously and has no impact or relevance in the way we live. This horrifying catalogue of despair is not the product of a disillusioned and darkened mind but is the clear verdict of your own Scriptures which you claim to know.

Everyone knows that God's directions, originally, are addressed to those who are born Jews so it follows that Jews have no excuse when it comes to living faultlessly by those rules and regulations. However, in reality, Jews are as incapable as everyone else of getting into a right relationship with God by obeying to the letter what is required of them by God. In fact, as they try, they become aware of the imperfection of their humanity like the rest of us.

So far, what I have written to you has been bad news leaving you, no doubt, depressed, miserable, and in the dark. I have been saying that God is not only our Creator, He is our Judge. That is absolutely true, but it leaves us high and dry so far as a hope and a future for us are concerned. Men and women are left completely bereft of a solution. But now for the Good News – God takes the initiative and has made us aware in history that there is another way into having a living relationship with Him which is not based on legal requirements.

The new relationship on which God accepts us is not on the basis that we are living a perfectly good life without flaw or failure; or keeping the Commandments that He has given; or following exactly and always the moral law which is within every human being. God's solution is achieved not BY faith but THROUGH faith. We can get into a right relationship with God through faith in Jesus Christ. It is never our faith that saves, redeems, and gives us hope in the midst of the darkness of our despair – it is Jesus who does that!

Now His salvation; His righteousness; His wisdom; His power; His holiness can become mine through faith in Him. Literally, there is no hope or future for any of us – religious or pagan – apart from Him and apart from this amazing, undeserved, and unearned initiative of God. In God's sight there are absolutely no distinctions. We are all in the same boat!! No matter how well we live or how high our standards are, we never make it into the unblemished splendour and unmeasurable greatness of God. Sin will forever exact its penalty on us – death; exert its power over us – slavery; and emit its pollution upon us – making us soiled.

I want to pick up on these three things that God sees – and deals with – as the consequences of sin. So far as the penalty of sin is concerned God acquits us; dismisses our case; declares us to be innocent (although we are guilty!). By the free gift of God's sheer, undeserved generosity and favour all can be put right with Him because of His dynamic and dramatic rescue act in sending His Son to be our substitute.

So far as the power of sin is concerned as it enslaves, controls, and captures us making us know the right but do the wrong; wanting the best but having to settle for the second best or worse; again Jesus is the only One who can set us free with the freedom which He alone can bring. By the sheer, undeserved generosity of God His Son not only secures forgiveness for our sin but makes freedom from sin a realistic possibility by giving us His Spirit to enable us to do right (I want to write about this more fully later).

There is so much more that God has done for us by His Son, Jesus. To help you understand the magnificence and magnitude of it all I have used the language of the law-court (justified), and the language of the slave-market (redemption) and now I want to use the language of the Temple (atonement through faith in His blood).

Jesus, gloriously, not only deals with the penalty and the power of sin, but also with the pollution of sin. Sin makes us dirty, soiled and contaminated in body, soul and spirit. The blood of Jesus, however, goes on cleansing us from all sin. You will quickly understand this wonderful concept because of your familiarity with the sacrificial system of ritual cleansing in the Temple. Having shared all this wonderful stuff with you, there is a huge question that requires an answer before we move on – how can God treat a bad man as if he were good and at the same time maintain His authority and integrity as a good, just, and righteous God?

Everybody knows that there are two things a good judge can never do – he cannot condemn those who are innocent and he cannot acquit those who are guilty. In answer to that, this is why Jesus is crucial and central to the Good News that I have been commissioned to declare because, when he was crucified on the Cross, God publicly and unmistakeably punished sin and was able personally and perfectly to pardon the sinner because He was in Christ reconciling the world to Himself.

Wonder of wonders God Himself bore our sin on Calvary's hill! That is why God cannot deal with sin apart from the death of His Son, Jesus, on the Cross. Jesus was God made flesh for our salvation!! So the penalty for sin has been paid; the power of sin has been broken; and the pollution by sin has been forever cleansed.

So, what do you make of all that? There is not an inch of ground left for us to stand on feeling proud, special, and unique. The big questions that still remain for us are: 'How can I get into God's good books?' 'How can I be sure that I am right with God?' 'How can I know that my destiny is heaven at the last?'

Clearly, doing good isn't the answer because we can never be absolutely sure that we have done enough good. Being religious isn't the answer because we can never be sure that we are religious enough or even that we are embracing the right religion. The only guarantee of acceptance, security, and hope that we have is through faith in what God has done in Jesus. This is an entirely new way to get right with God; not through the privileges of race or the practice of religion but through the principle of faith! Notice that removes forever any superiority or inferiority feelings.

I realise this is so hard for you to accept because we may never have done anything considered to be good all through our lives, or we may never have allowed a day to pass without doing something good, but neither gets you put right with God. In other words, good works will never get you into heaven and bad works need not keep you out of heaven. Let me say to you again that it is not our race or our religion or our pedigree that count. There is only one God and there is only one way to get right with that God – and that is the same way for the Jew and the non-Jew. I can almost hear you asking: 'Does this mean that the Law of God is discarded; destroyed and overthrown?' Absolutely not!!!

I will deal with this question more fully later on in this letter, but in the meantime I want you to realise that our faith is in Someone who upheld the Law and kept it perfectly; Someone who accepted the penalty of the Law and died to pay that penalty as is legally required; Someone who fills my heart with His love, and that love fulfils the Law and makes me want to honour it. You see, when you are living by the principle of faith you want to keep the Law, not because you will be punished if you don't, but because you love the God who gave it and you want to do what you know He wants you to do.

~CHAPTER 4~

Let me try and put some flesh on all of this for you for faith is such an abstract concept and is best understood when displayed and demonstrated in people. It occurs to me that Abraham would be a good example of what I am teaching since he is so deeply respected by those of us who are Jews as the founder, and as the father of our race. How did he get right with God?

It wasn't because he was an extraordinarily good man who did good things. In fact he was deceitful and told lies!! He became God's friend when he stood at the door of his tent one night and saw 6,000 stars with his naked eye and God said to him that his descendants were going to be as many as the stars in the sky (although he was a frail old man and Sarah, his wife, could no longer conceive a child because of her age!).

Abraham responded to God in faith and said: 'God, I believe you because I know that You will always, without fail, do what You say.' Right living did not make him right with God – faith did! You see, God 'spells' the word righteousness as F.A.I.T.H. As a result Abraham could never claim superiority over anyone. God owed him nothing, and he owed God everything. God not only accepts my faith instead of right living but He also abolishes my guilt through faith.

Let's move forward a bit in history to a thousand years ago when your great forebear, King David, discovered and declared the same thing. You would certainly know that in one act he broke five of God's Commandments. No wonder he sings about our God who looks on our faith rather than the awesome blunders of our lives. Wrongs are forgiven; sins are pardoned. God deals with our sinfulness in such a way that we will never be held to account for it. No wonder King David is lyrical about faith. Do you really understand what I am saying? It is clearly taught and demonstrated in the Scriptures that what we have been taught is the clear and unchangeable Word of God.

In view of all that I have written about Abraham and David you could have the impression that all this applies to Jews only. Let me say right away that this would be a wrong conclusion. You need to look at the historical circumstances and ask the question: 'When was Abraham put right with God – before or after he was circumcised (one of the main seals and signs of Judaism)? Clearly he had this dramatic encounter with God outside the tent looking up into the starry sky fourteen years before he was circumcised. It was not the ceremonial ritual that put him right with God – it was faith! Circumcision was a physical, visible evidence on his body that he had already been put right with God.

The consequence of this historical investigation is that our security and hope do not lie in some religious rite or ceremony, but in faith in what God says – not in what we do. In the light of this, Abraham is the father of both Jews and non-Jews. It is faith that makes me a son of Abraham and not circumcision.

Be assured, then, that the promise of God has nothing to do with the Law since the Law was given 400 years after God made a covenant and commitment to Abraham. Our godly inheritance comes not through what we do with our hands but through what and how we hear with our ears. If our future inheritance depends on what we do and how we perform then faith is worthless and God's promise is empty. Those who attempt to earn their salvation find themselves the recipients of God's awesome judgment because to live by the Law is to be judged by the Law. To exchange Law for the sheer, undeserved and unearned generosity of God is to be freed from the penalty of sin.

It is important for you to know that Abraham had two kinds of descendants; those who have his blood in them from generation to generation and those who do not have his blood in them. But God's promise is to both because both share his faith not his blood. So far as God is concerned Abraham's faith rests on the fact that God can create something out of nothing – otherwise his child, Isaac, would not have been born. His faith is also focused on the reality that God can resurrect life out of death – since Isaac was as good as dead so far as Abraham was concerned when he took him, in obedience to God, up Mount Moriah to make him a sacrifice.

This is the same God we believe in who sent His Son, Jesus, into the world supernaturally and against scientific possibility by being born of a virgin and then reached into the tomb on Easter morning and resurrected that same Son. These are the two pivotal realities upon which our faith rests in the same way that Abraham's did.

It was totally inconceivable to Abraham, in the natural realm, that he would become what God said he would become internationally and universally. He faced the fact fairly and squarely that naturally there was not the remotest possibility that he and his wife Sarah would become parents. Yet resolutely and unquestioningly he said to God, "I believe You".

The result was that he confidently grasped the unseen as if it were seen; the intangible as if it were tangible; the eternal as if it were historical; and the divine as if it were human and worshipped and praised God for who He is and for what he would do. The darkness and destructiveness of doubt did not enter his mind for his focus was entirely on God who not only makes promises but unfailingly keeps them. This is what it takes to get right with God.

There is no other way for any of us at any time to enter into a living and vibrant relationship with God other than to believe implicitly and unwaveringly that our God moved into the darkness and seeming finality of the tomb and healed, restored, and re-created the broken, suffocated and lifeless body of His Son, Jesus our Master, and brought Him out with a completely new body as the first-born of His new Creation in perfection and power. This is where our faith must be focused; on what God has done for us in His Incarnate Son, who paid the penalty for our sin in His death and gave us unbounded and eternal hope by His life. I want so much to settle in your minds what faith really is so that I can go on to speak to you about where and in Whom our faith is to rest and remain.

∾ CHAPTER 5 ∾

Because of all this wonderful stuff there is a profound difference in my status – in the past my credit-rating was light and my debts were heavy but now my credit-rating in inexhaustible and my debts are non-existent. The fact is that where I was wrong with God, now I am right with God. Oh, I do realise that this can seem like mental juggling with words; a conceptual, cerebral theology that really doesn't touch down in reality. I want you to know that nothing could be further from the truth since there are positive, personal, and practical consequences – not only is my status different but my state is different too.

For the first time in my life there is no hostility whatsoever between me and my Creator. You see, before we believed – in the same way that Abraham believed – we did not like God's Word or God's people. We did not like being reminded of God, and deep down in our hearts we were still afraid of the punishment of God. But now all that is changed. This is not simply personal and self-indulgent but it is actually the foundational key to the conflicts and confrontations of our world.

You know perfectly well from your Scriptures (in the Book of Beginnings called Genesis) that to get out of a right relationship with God quickly and inevitably leads to getting out of a right relationship with our fellow human beings. Presumably, then, to get into a right relationship with God will quickly and inevitably lead to getting into a right relationship with all those around us. This signals the end of our ongoing, endless search for peace in our time – what we are looking for is not finding a formula that will enable us to have peace with one another but finding a faith that will enable us to have peace with God.

This must now be our cry to the world – faith not formula!! This not only becomes possible but is, in fact, real because of what our Master, Saviour, and Anointed One sent from God has done. But, amazingly, we not only have peace with God but we also have admission to the royal court of heaven where we have an undeserved and unlimited audience with the Creator and the Sustainer of the whole universe. Jesus ushers us into the very presence of God as He opens the door for us to the King of Kings where we find neither condemnation nor judgment but the sheer, undeserved, unearned, unmerited, incredible kindness and favour of God.

As if that were not enough there is still more – no wonder words fail us and our cup is overflowing! Faith looks back at what God has undoubtedly and perfectly done but since we have been put right with God there is something we can look forward to in the future as well. This is not wishful thinking or vacuous day-dreaming but it is absolute certainty.

We can now look forward to leaving the land of the dying and entering forever the land of the living where darkness, sadness, sickness, pain, parting, sorrow, heart-break will never again be our experience. Then and there I will be given a new body which will resemble the resurrection body of Jesus Himself; my character will be perfected; and my new dwelling place will be exactly right for me because the New Creation will have been completed.

However, that is then, but what about right now? At this present time in Rome you are under the pressure of your circumstances and constantly confronted by pain and persecution. You can react in one of three ways – you can rebel against it and become bitter and resentful; you can resign yourself to it in a despairing and fatalistic passivity; or you can rejoice over it because you know deep down in your spirit that it is not negative and destructive but rather it is positive and creative. You need not sit down under it but you can tackle it head-on and use it to be like metal which has been passed through the fire purging it of the alloy of baseness and producing sterling reality.

There is always the danger that when the going gets really tough we begin to think that God doesn't love us anymore; doesn't care for us anymore; and has lost interest in us and so we lose heart and eventually lose hope. Of course, that is very natural and completely understandable. So we need the supernatural to break into our lives in extravagant and overflowing measure. That is precisely what God does in these circumstances. His Holy Spirit enables us to behave not in a natural or an unnatural way, but in an entirely supernatural way. It is because of this, whatever happens, that we can face the present and the future with faith rather than with fear.

To be a Christian is not a hobby or an interest or an optional extra to our lives – it is a matter of life and death. In fact the process is reversed – it is a matter of death and life – Christ living in order to die (for us!) and our dying in order to live (for Him!). God's timing is always perfect although we live with our eyes on a different clock. You know perfectly well that goodness attracts us and makes us want to do the best we can and give the most we can (even being willing to surrender our lives and future) for someone we respect, honour, love, and admire. But Jesus was vastly different, giving His life for those who disregarded God; defied the Laws of God; and lived soiled and unworthy lives. To put it very bluntly, Jesus died for bad people. Be assured of this that Christianity is the only religion that was born in a cemetery.

The glorious fact is that I have been put right with God because of what Jesus, His Son, did when He died on the Cross on the hill of Calvary outside Jerusalem. As a result God's inevitable and just punishment for sin has been forever dealt with through faith in that same Jesus. But there is even more to it than that for Jesus not only died for me while I was living without Him and was intensely hostile to Him, but He is living now, having defeated death, and He goes on helping me on a daily basis.

He wants to be my substitute in a double way in that He not only wanted to die on my behalf, He wants also to live in my place – so His life in me confronts my constant struggle with temptation; my bewilderment when life collapses in on me; and my vulnerability when I cannot cope with life's difficulties and dangers. It really is staggering to realise that we have a Saviour who died that we might be reconciled to God, but we also have a risen Lord who lives that we might rejoice in God whatever life throws at us.

I am aware that you might well be asking, how can the death of someone who died a great distance from you, and some years before you, really affect you in such a radical way? You must know from your Scriptures that someone who lived many centuries before Christ radically affected your life because of his blatant disobedience and folly – his name was Adam. However strange and even offensive this might be to you, the fact is we are all part of one human race. We are all bound up together and what affects one in some way and at some time will affect all.

This is really difficult for us to grasp because, as human beings, we feel so deeply that what we do is our own, personal business and has nothing whatsoever to do with anyone else. Actually, the reverse of that is the reality of the situation – what I do profoundly affects other people either positively or negatively. As human beings, our lives certainly are personal but they are never private. You see, God made man to live forever, but one man (Adam) spoiled that. Evil did not originate in this world – it started outside and came into it infecting it as long as human history lasts.

It was among the angels that rebellion against God first started, and the leader of this group of proud, rebellious angels introduced sin into this world. He required a human being to accomplish his purposes, and he found that person in the historical figure on earth of Adam. You need to understand that long before Moses received God's rules and regulations for His People, sin was already present. Of course, God's rules defined right and wrong for the Jewish people and prior to that sin was not clearly defined. But a new phenomenon was now introduced into the world the moment Adam disregarded God's instructions in the Garden of Eden – death!!

At that moment of disobedience Adam's body began to die, and from then until now we have all had to face that fearful enemy – death. Sin is a universal problem and so requires a universal rescue plan because everyone on the face of the earth, in every generation, not only has followed Adam's example and repeated his folly, but everyone has inherited his nature. This is a profoundly deep and disturbing reality that physically we were in Adam's body as he is in our bodies; but spiritually when Adam sinned the whole human race that was to come sinned too!

There is no comparison between what Adam did and what Jesus did – one led to retribution and fear; the other led to restoration and redemption. You need to understand what I am saying – that all of the human race was in Adam (our human forebear) and when he sinned we all sinned and came to inherit death. This is how the human race works. Adam's disobedience has affected us all! But here is the incredible Good News that because of another Man's obedience and absolute submission to God at a specific place called Calvary, outside Jerusalem, and at a specific time in history, everyone relating to Him through faith is now declared righteous. What a magnificent rescue-plan!!

∼ CHAPTER 6 ∼

All that I have just written could, so easily, lead us to be faced with a very foolish, human pre-occupation – jumping to the wrong conclusion. There are those who have concluded in the light of all that has just been said that, therefore, it doesn't matter how you live if it is true that no matter how good you are, or how bad you are, you have been saved by God's sheer, undeserved generosity alone through faith in the Lord Jesus Christ.

On this basis, they say, the greater the sin the greater the sheer, undeserved generosity of God is released. If living a good life did not count before I became a Christian, then living a careless, irresponsible, God-forgetting life after I have become a Christian is of no consequence. Surely this would give God an opportunity to demonstrate how lavish and unfathomable His generosity really is. Let me confront that wrong conclusion now. Hear what I am saying, Christian, and hear it with absolute clarity – nothing could be further from the truth than that!!

Be completely assured it is not true that because our sin is comprehensively dealt with through the lavish, extravagant, and undeserved generosity of God then sinning is a good thing because it demonstrates the incredible nature of God. The reality is that God has shown that the opposite of bad, so far as He is concerned, is not good but grace. I want you to grasp a new principle, and once you have grasped this it will lead you in a completely new way of living.

Here, then, is the principle – to be a Christian you need not go on sinning after you have been converted. Notice, it is not a question of cannot but a question of need not. That is the glorious good news that, as Christians, we often miss. You see, when you were baptized, you attended your own funeral service. Whether you realise it, or felt it, or not, at your conversion God put you into Christ and particularly into His death and resurrection. So, when Jesus died on the Cross on the hill of Calvary, so did you. In other words, what happened to Him, happened to you.

26

The staggering thing is that after a person dies he is out of the reach of the law so that it cannot punish him; he is also out of the reach of sin so that it cannot soil him; and he is out of the reach of Satan so that he cannot touch him. The reality is that as with Christ, so it is with us. How glorious and magnificent is that? This is the thrilling and profound meaning of baptism – burial is taking place; the body is being put out of sight; death has occurred. It is not so much what you were baptized IN that matters but WHO/WHAT you were baptized into.

But God not only put us into the death of Christ, but also into His resurrection. Obviously you know that when Jesus rose from the tomb where He was buried He never went to, spoke with, nor had anything to do with Pilate, the Roman Governor who allowed Him to be executed, nor with Annas and Caiaphas, the High Priests who condemned Him, nor with any of the priests, the soldiers, the Pharisees, or indeed Satan. You see, He had finished with that old life and now He only dealt with God and God's people. So it is with you – you have, in Christ, died to all that was part of your old life and you have risen to a completely new life.

Dearest friends, if you are able to grasp this principle you have grasped the releasing, liberating secret of overcoming and conquering evil. It is pure bluff when the seductive, beguiling, persuasive Satan speaks to you because you are now dead to him, and he need not ensnare you. Of course, he will do his utmost to convince you that you are still a victim of his power and under his control to make you sin. Not true!! You are alive now only to God.

There is no need for you any longer to try to get into a state of victory over sin – you are already there! It is a fruitless and frustrating exercise for you to try to conquer sin – Christ has already done that for you! You may be asking the question. 'Is this not self-deception? Am I not simply bluffing myself into thinking that I am now free not to sin?' By no means! In fact the reverse is true – it is Satan who is bluffing us in attempting to persuade and convince us that we are still very much alive to sin. No!! A thousand times no – you are dead to sin.

I cannot leave you still wondering about this! Apply the principle of Christ's death and resurrection first of all to your mind and then to your body. Spiritual revelation without practical, physical response is dead. So, feed your mind with these crucial and fundamental facts of the Good News of God – Christ has died, Christ is risen. Nothing that earth or hell can do can alter these facts. Our feelings have no part to play in this.

Apply your mind to this – the old you is dead; new life has come!! Now back this up with your body. In your old life you gave parts of your body and emotions to Satan – your eyes, your ears, your mouth, your hands, your feet, your feelings. He used your body – your human-ness. Don't let him boss you anymore. Grasp the principle with your mind that you have died with Christ; been buried with Him; and now you are risen to new life with Him. Now practice refusing to allow Satan to use any part of your humanity. This is where the Holy Spirit wants to come alongside us to encourage and enable us.

Does this mean that I am finished with obeying the Law now? Can I do what I like now – even doing what I know to be wrong? Never!! You see, some people only hear that they are now no longer under law but entirely miss the fact that they are now under grace. It is true that you are no longer under law – but you are under something else! This is a new relationship that requires a new response.

O dear Roman Christians, surely you, of all people, know that submission to someone as a slave – even if it is a voluntary submission – means that you are obedient to that person without any questions being asked or quarter being given. If your submission is to your own selfish desires or to a blatant disregard for God then the unmitigated consequence is eternal death and everlasting darkness. If, on the other hand, your submission is to the unearned favour and lavish generosity of

God the consequence is an unhindered and life-transforming relationship with Him.

The former is where you used to be, but with unspeakable gratitude to God the latter is where you are now. You are in a relationship now which makes continuing to sin and living entirely for yourself absolutely unthinkable. Let me use a human illustration with which you are familiar – when you chose the Lord (or responded to His choice of you!) you chose to be His slave. You did not sign a new contract but you submitted to a new commitment. God did not set you free to do what you like; He set you free to do what He likes.

When you were a slave of sin you were free to behave badly, but now you are a slave to do good in a way that pleases God and so you are no longer free to do evil. In a word, you have exchanged one slavery for another and one master for another. There was a day when you submitted your humanity to live with unclean thoughts and actions, and you discovered that godlessness and unworthy living escalated beyond your ability to control it. You were a powerless captive to sin. Now reverse this process by becoming a powerful captive to good-living and God-pleasing.

When you were a captive to sin you were never bothered nor convicted by the way you were living. But think back – was there any value in living that way now that you have another perspective for living? You are now aware – although you did not recognise it then – that the destiny of that kind of life is eternal disaster. However, everything has fundamentally and radically changed because you have a new Master who wants to give you a life worth living and a destiny that is beyond your ability to imagine or understand.

In case you are feeling depressed and discouraged by what I am saying – that is, you are still not free because you have exchanged one master for another – you need to realise the kind of Master you now have. You are living there at the heart of the Roman Empire and you know that the Roman soldier gets his wages – he has earned what he gets; and an agreement has been reached about what he gets. If sin is your master you get what you deserve – death.

We kill our bodies through sin by living in a careless, irresponsible and harmful way. We also kill our minds through sin allowing suspicion, criticism, spitefulness, jealousy, and impurity to dominate our thinking. Most devastating of all we kill our spirits through sin so that we have no awareness of God's presence and no pleasure among God's people and our sense of wonder is strangled at birth. These are the wages sin doles out, for death always results from sin being our master. However, you also know that a Roman soldier, from time to time, gets a free gift – on the Emperor's birthday; or when the Emperor visits his legion; or when a crucial military victory is celebrated. In other words it is a bonus for which he has actually done nothing.

Some masters only give their slaves what they work for and what they have earned. Other masters give unearned, extra gifts to their slaves. Your new Master doesn't pay wages at all, He only gives a free gift – something you can never work for nor earn – eternal life. O my Roman friends, you need to know that there is no such thing as freedom in this world – we are all slaves to someone or to something. In fact, those who claim to be free are normally those who are most in bondage. It is true that you have changed masters – but which would you rather work for?

∽ CHAPTER 7 ∽

Often when a Christian sins he does so because he is not fully aware of what has happened to him as a Christian. That is why I am using two illustrations from earthly relationships. I have already spoken of the relationship between master and slave which you obviously know so well. Now I want to speak to you about another significant relationship – the relationship between husband and wife.

30

You see, a Christian needs to add knowledge to his faith for one of the things that will keep him from sinning is knowledge. This is the reason I am using these two physical and social illustrations to help you understand a basic spiritual principle about law and grace. Let me apply the significance spiritually of this social, physical relationship of marriage.

Surely you must realise that to be married is to be totally and exclusively committed to one person. Of course, we are not married for eternity but only for time. Marriage begins with a wedding and ends with a funeral. The law demands that you can only be married to one person at a time. To marry another while your partner is still alive is to be guilty of adultery. A woman cannot change partners unless and until her husband dies. However, within an hour of her husband's death she can marry another without breaking the law – but not an hour before his death!

The fact is that you were married to the Law of God, and you found that to be demanding, exacting, and difficult to honour and obey. But, my dear Family of God, you died in Christ when He died on the Cross and so you have been set free from your first husband. You need to know, however, that the very act that set you free from the first marriage to the Law bound you to Christ because the Church is the Bride of Christ. Your new Husband is alive, and through His risen life within us by the Holy Spirit we are to give visible evidence of this invisible but unbelievably real relationship.

Please notice that this marriage is not just for time alone but for eternity because Jesus will never die again. Notice also that some marriages, in the human context, bring out the worst in each partner while other marriages bring out the best in each partner. Now you cherish your new husband as the Bride of Christ, and you are now living His risen life by the Holy Spirit who brings out life rather than death; hope rather than despair; and light rather than darkness. You see, your new Husband doesn't give wages, He gives gifts and brings out the best, not the worst, in you. In a word, the Christian can now be free from sin – but he is not free to sin!

In all of this we have hit a problem – you could conclude that the Law of God is evil. Nothing could be further from the truth. Let me affirm as clearly and as concisely as I can that the Law is divine and has within it the very voice of God. It settles all relationships, both human and divine, and had it been able to be perfectly and absolutely kept it would ensure that we would be in a perfect relationship both with God and with our fellowman. It was designed for nothing other than our highest welfare.

The Law was meant to make bad people good. Yet the fact remains that that same Law can be the very thing through which sin gains entry into us. Let me explain how this can be. The Law defines sin. Until a thing is defined as sin by the Law, we cannot know that it is sin. In that sense, sin without the Law has no existence. Let me share my own testimony of my spiritual journey.

I had learned to control my actions and words, but to control my thoughts, feelings and emotions was a quite different matter. Nine of the Commandments have to do with actions and words – there is an outwardness about them. But the tenth Commandment is inward and has to do with thoughts and feelings. I did not fully realise this until I read Exodus, Chapter 20 and verse 17 and Deuteronomy, Chapter 5 and verse 21. That did it! I was lost! I was defeated! I was powerless!

I realised that covetousness – this longing, this craving, this jealous eagerness to possess something (especially the property of another person – his goods; his relationships; his standing; his reputation) was the sin of sins; it gave birth to every other sin. I was cornered and helpless.

To make matters worse the terrible paradox gripped me that my realisation of this prohibition spawned the very sin which it forbade. It was in and through this very Commandment that sin found its opportunity. It awakened and brought to life the very sin which it sought to suppress. You see, our human nature very quickly responds that when a thing is forbidden it becomes amazingly desirable. In this case what a person may not have – became the very thing that above all he desired to have.

One of the strange facts of life is the fascination of the forbidden thing. The very Commandment that God intended to bring freedom and life brought

32

bondage and death. This is not a criticism of the Law but the condemnation of my human nature. So this holy, righteous and good Law points out sin to me; provokes my beguiled, flawed human nature to sin; and makes me aware that my deepest need is not reformation (because I am powerless to do anything about it myself) but regeneration through the powerful, transforming Holy Spirit and redemption through the incredible reality of a crucified Saviour.

All of this can become very confusing. It can seem that what is pure, undefiled, just and blameless causes me to confront darkness, destruction and death. That is certainly not true and we must never come to that conclusion! Rather, the awfulness of sin is seen by the fact that it can take a fine thing that is godly and good and make it an instrument of evil. The very fact that sin took the Law of God and made it a bridgehead to sin shows so conclusively and disturbingly the supreme sinfulness of sin. The whole terrible process is not accidental; it is all designed to show us how awful a thing sin is, because it can take the loveliest and noblest of things and defile them with its polluting touch.

You and I both know that the Law of God has God's voice in it and that it comes out of eternity into history and out of heaven into earth. The problem is I am so anchored in history rather than eternity and so earth-bound rather than heaven-focused that I am controlled and captivated by my sinful human nature. I am really at a loss to grasp what is going on inside me. I know what is right and good and godly, and I really do want to embrace that by living accordingly, and yet, somehow, I can't and I don't!! It leaves me feeling frustrated, soiled and guilty.

I cannot explain my perverse and inexplicable behaviour since I want to honour God. I know what is wrong, and the last thing I want is to respond to it – but I do!! I have come to the conclusion that though I cannot avoid taking responsibility for the way I behave, this dilemma that I face is caused by my flawed, failing and yet demanding sinful human nature. I so much want to do the right thing and live a God-pleasing life but I can't. I have the ability to recognize what is wrong but I am haunted by my failure to resist it. I can only conclude that there is another force; another power; another drive at work within me. Knowledge is not enough; theology can't cut it; discipline can't deliver.

Please forgive me for baring my soul and writing so openly to you. I have come to see the inadequacy of human knowledge. If to know the right thing is to do it I would be free – but I am not! Human knowledge by itself cannot make me good. I have come to see, too, the inadequacy of human resolution. Will-power has very severe limitations! I have also come to see the limitations of human diagnosis. I see so clearly what is wrong, but I don't know how to fix it.

There is a civil war being waged deep inside me. I am a man who is totally exhausted, spent and helpless. Who is there to rescue me from this fatal body that answers so comprehensively and destructively to the seductions of sin? Morality and religion cannot help me – for I have tried (oh, how I have tried!) so hard and I have failed. But, oh, blessing, and honour, and praise, and gratitude be to God – He has provided a way by sending His Anointed One to be our perfect Saviour and triumphant, risen, reigning Lord!!

Without God's rescue plan I have no hope and no future because God's perfect Law defies my ability to fulfil it.

∽ CHAPTER 8 ∽

So then, in the light of all that I have written to you in this Letter, you can be absolutely convinced and content that now God sees us as He sees His own Son, Jesus, clean and pure and free from the awesomeness of God's judgment because we have been clothed and covered by the perfection, obedience and holiness of the sinless Son of God. We are no longer dominated by the domineering and death-delivering demands of our fallen human nature.

We have a new Master who dictates the road we should walk; the way we should live; and the paths we should choose. He is the Father-glorifying, sin-exposing, joy-giving, love-imparting, relationship-building, holiness-encouraging, energy-releasing, truth-telling, witness-enabling, Gift-bearing, miracle-working, fruit-producing, power-providing, life-changing Spirit. Because of our God-resisting, self-centred, temptation-seduced human nature God's Law was impotent to accomplish what it set out to do. God had to bring us to that place of recognising our own helplessness and hopelessness so that we cried out for help.

God was not deaf to our often unspoken cry and so He sent His own Son, bone of our bone and flesh of our flesh, to become our Saviour. It is only as we gaze at the Cross on the hill of Calvary and what Jesus did there that we can begin to understand the sinfulness of sin and the utter helplessness of our humanity to respond to the holiness of God. No wonder that the Good news of Jesus can only be described as wonder upon wonder and every wonder true because our old proud, grace-resistant, self-promoting humanity has been replaced by the God-honouring, Christ-exalting Spirit.

It is all a question of focus – if our attention is absorbed by our earth-bound, self-promoting human nature then that is the way we will live; but if our attention is absorbed by God-longings and Christ-pleadings then our behaviour will be entirely transformed. That is why the Holy Spirit came – to transform us into God-honouring, Kingdom people.

Make no mistake your mind dictates how you live and a mind dominated by godless, greedy, grasping, lustful, self-gratifying thoughts, motives and intentions will land up in a hopeless grave in the end. However, the mind that is mastered and submitted to the Spirit of the living God, will take us into living as God always intended and discovering a sense of well-being and wholeness we could never have dreamed of or imagined.

You see, when our minds are beguiled by temptation and seduced by sin, we instinctively resist God and despise His truth. In a word, we are absolutely powerless to do what we were created to do – to please God and enjoy Him forever.

I realise that is not where you are coming from. You have discovered that Calvary is not simply on a hill far away but is a vital reality in your heart; and the empty, borrowed, rock-hewn tomb is not only located in an eastern garden, but is the powerful, resurrection reality of your own life-experience so that the Jesus-life has assuredly been born in you. Of course, you are part of a fallen creation, corrupted by sin, and so physical death will one day take you to an earthly grave. But a new life has been born in you that can and will never die because of the God-pleasing, sin-cleansing life, death and resurrection of Jesus that completely satisfied the unalterable holiness of God.

Oh, brothers and sisters, how can I write this without bursting into inexpressible song – the very same power that reached into the sealed and guarded tomb of Jesus and brought Him out in glorious resurrection power will one day reach into the grave where your body will rest and bring it out into a new resurrection morning. Spirit and body – separated at physical death – will be reunited and you, too, will have a new, eternal, glorious body like His, that will never again die because the Spirit of the living God is eternal.

Brothers and sisters, the options are clear – life or death; hope or despair; light or darkness; blessing or curse. It all depends on who is pulling your strings, you or God!!

Hear the cry of my heart – "Make the right choice!" – for God wants you to be in the Family where he is Father. You were never destined to be depersonalized, isolated captives to a cruel and ruthless master, quivering at the thought of justice and punishment. You were born into a Family – the Family of God – when you became Christians by the radical, life-transforming, regenerating Spirit of the living God. God always intended intimacy with Himself for you so that you would know the warmth, tenderness, and security of His embrace.

This reality goes beyond reason, feelings, and any outward sign and is a transforming certainty deep within our very being. Only God can do this – and he has! Since this is true then our inheritance is massive. It is totally beyond our comprehension and soars out of history into eternity and breaks free from the human into the divine. There is a cost to be paid, however, for all that breaks God's heart now breaks ours. But there is no doubt at all about the final outcome – the radiant brightness of His character and the comprehensive and limitless fullness of His being will be seen.

What is happening to us now, with its pain and heartbreak, bears no resemblance whatsoever to the comprehensive and limitless fullness of God radiating out from us in a coming day. What is hidden now will be revealed in that day. The world around us, that we know so well, is standing on tiptoe to see who's who in redemption reality.

Man's disobedience in the beginning had global implications, for everything around him was affected. Ever since, the created world around us has never had its longings and its hopes satisfied because of demonic vindictiveness. But in that day, too, the created world around us will burst forth from its cycle of life that ends in death, and the constantly recurring sadness of a Spring that ultimately ends in Winter and will share the indescribable liberty of those who have been redeemed and released by the blood of Jesus Christ.

Since the fatal Fall in the Garden of Eden all of the created world around us has endured the struggles, pain, and discomfort of the pregnant mother waiting for her time to come. In a similar way we, too, who have tasted the initial realities of Kingdom living, silently cry from the depths of our being as we anticipate, with unashamed enthusiasm, the ultimate evidence of who we really are – our Christ-resembling, resurrection-perfect, death-defeated bodies.

This is what has kept us going since the time God rescued and redeemed us. This is reality, but it is not yet! We claim it by the faith which makes the invisible visible; the intangible tangible; and the not-yet now. That is what makes our anticipation vibrantly resilient, relentlessly enduring, and unbreakably strong.

We are so aware of our mortality and humanity now, but God has not left us to our own devices to stumble and stagger along by ourselves. He has come alongside us to help us in our vulnerability and frailty by His Spirit. It is incredible that even as we try to handle the mystery of prayer He does our praying in us and for us when all we're capable of is wordless sounds. He not only knows us better than we know ourselves but keeps us present before God – and here is the result; the reality of God's will becomes the longing of our hearts.

Would you notice something with a new clarity? Everything will not work for good for you simply because God loves you (although His love for you is unmistakably real!). You will need to love Him too and demonstrate the reality of your love by fulfilling His calling upon your life in a glad and eager obedience. There is a human as well as a divine side in all of this. This is not a threat – it is a relationship thing; and that is what Christianity is all about.

Grasp this and life begins to take on an entirely new harmony. Instead of some things which are bad (in my estimation) and some things which are good – life becomes a harmony. I no longer have to struggle and worry about avoiding the unpleasant and grasping the pleasant. God is on the throne of the universe and is magnificently reigning and gloriously in control. He can take what we perceive to be the worst possible scenario and make it the best in His eternal purposes.

Please realise that God knew all about us even before He had created the universe. I am here and I am now by choice and not by chance. God chose us so that He might have a Family and His Son might have many brothers and sisters. In order to do this He had to forgive all my past and all my future sins. But God never begins a job without completing it and seeing it right through to the end. You see, God can talk of the future as if it were completed.

Here is your security – you began in eternity with God's choice and you end in eternity with God's glory. Your security – from beginning to end – depends on God and not on you!! Here is how it works – God chose you and set you apart before there was a universe; God called you in the midst of the years; God put you right with Himself through the triumph of Calvary; and God shared His glory with you. It is all God's work. Your security depends on God's sovereignty. It is not your hold on Him that keeps you secure; it's His hold on you!

In view of all of this, what do you say? This is a God-thing we are dealing with here. Nobody and nothing is a match for God! Who can stop the process of salvation from being completed? Who can deny you your glorified body? Who can stop God completing the job He has begun in your life? Nobody is in a position to accuse you anymore – conscience can't; the devil can't; people can't. They may all have good grounds for their accusations, but they are impotent.

There is no Counsel for the prosecution for God gave His own Son; so He will not charge you. In addition there is no Counsel for the defence for God has appointed His Son, Jesus, as Judge of the whole world; and the Judge is pleading for you. Nothing can keep us out of heaven. It is staggeringly wonderful that the promised Messiah, Jesus, not only died for us but now lives for us as we continue our earthly journey.

From the place of authority He opens His heart to the Father on our behalf. Be assured, however, that the Messiah is not only Judge but He is also the Lover of the souls of men – and nothing can wrestle us from that enduring and tenacious love. Affliction is powerless here; difficult and hard-to-understand circumstances can't; hostility towards us; natural disasters; and abject poverty won't. Frighteningly terrifying prospects and even the pain and darkness of death itself are neutralized in the presence of such love. All of this doesn't take us by surprise, because long ago we were warned that discipleship is costly and martyrdom and premature death may well be the consequence of radical and absolute commitment to Jesus.

Let me re-affirm and emphasize that all these things are not defeat but rather triumph because of the transforming love of the Saviour, Jesus. There is not a shadow of doubt in my mind that in life we live with Christ; in death we die with Him; and because we die with Him, we also rise with Him – so living or dying we are in a win-win situation.

God's love is unaffected by supernatural beings – both good or bad. The day will come when this world will be dissolved and the new age of God's perfect glory will dawn. It makes no difference whatsoever – when the world, as we know it, has gone and God's new creation has come the creative, enduring, resilient security of His love will still be the same.

Malign influences in whatever shape or form they come cannot create a chasm between us and the lavish limitlessness of God's love. The stars cannot hurt, influence or affect you, for they, too, are powerless to separate you from God's love. Even if by some wild flight of your imagination, there emerged another and different world, you would still be safe, enwrapped by the love of God. So, think of every terrifying thing that this or any other world can produce, and be absolutely certain and secure that not one of them is able to separate the Christian from the love of God that is in Christ Jesus; for He is Lord of every terror and Master of every world.

～ CHAPTER 9 ～

However, having written what I have just written, I want to confront some big issues with you. Undoubtedly, you will struggle with some of the things I say to you because I want to speak of God as He is and not God as we would like Him to be. It's not so much your understanding of what I am saying that will cause you difficulty as it is your preferences and even your prejudices.

Your reason may well be offended because God intends and will require to manage your lives; and He insists on having a different perspective on life from yours. Consequently you will need to see things from His point of view and not yours. Please accept that what I am writing is true and that it comes from a pure and unsullied heart and has the imprimatur of God by His Spirit upon it. I have approached writing this part of my letter with an overwhelming and almost unbearable sadness and burden. I feel this so deeply, it is almost beyond my ability to put it into words.

You see, I am writing this with my Jewish kinsmen in mind, not from a position of pride or conceitedness but from a position of searing, devastating heart-brokenness. I would willingly exchange places with you, my precious blood-brothers, even if it meant that I would never again know the blessing and favour of God as I am now as a result of the sheer undeserved generosity and favour of God's heart.

From what I have just written it seems completely incongruous and contradictory what I am writing now. I have just said that when God chooses us He keeps us and nothing can separate us from His love. Yet it seems that my Jewish kinsmen have been separated from that love. Oh my Jewish brothers, you had it all – a unique relationship with God; a holy anointing from God; an unchangeable and clear commitment by God; access to straightforward rules for living in God; and precious assurances from God. This has continued from generation to generation through the honoured and chosen representatives of God showing an unbroken line to the Messiah who is God made flesh, recognised and exalted. Oh, endless hallelujahs!! Amen!!

Be absolutely sure that when God says something He means it. When God makes a promise He keeps it. We have so misunderstood what happened when God committed to the Jews – it is such a flawed, fundamental, and fatal misunderstanding. God never made His promises to all the Jews – only to some. It is so true that all could have shared His promises – but tragically they didn't. The physical descendants of Abraham do not all inherit God's promises. The children of Abraham to whom God's promises were given are not his physical children but his spiritual children; those who not only share his flesh and blood but also his faith.

Long ago, in the Book of Beginnings (known as Genesis) God clearly told Abraham that not all of his eight children would inherit His promises – only one, Isaac. Isaac alone had been born according to God's will and through God's supernatural power. It is a stark reminder that God's promises are only viable when we are in God's will. God made it abundantly and amazingly clear to both Abraham and Sarah that He would overcome the limitations of human reproduction, and the son they would produce would be the result of His supernatural favour.

This outworking of God's eternal and historical purposes would not be limited to one generation but would continue. Isaac and Rebekah had twin babies together, and according to human rules Esau should have inherited God's promise because he was slightly older than Isaac. But before they were born – before they had done anything and regardless of how they had lived – God had made His choice. You see, God has freewill just as we have. So added to your fearful conclusion that God is unfaithful to His promises is the unnerving concern that God is unfair in His dealings with His people.

What conclusion have you really reached? Are you really charging God with injustice and favouritism? Nothing can be further from the truth. Go back in your history to the epic story of Moses. Do you remember what He said to that distinguished and dynamic leader of His people? To say God is unfair is to be completely blind to the condition of humanity. Not a single person among us, past and present, deserves to be chosen by God. Frankly, it is not a matter of justice but of mercy that God chooses anyone.

No matter how deeply we yearn or how hard we try, we will never make it in the light of the absolute sinless and shadowless perfection of God and the deeply flawed and failed nature of men and women. Our only hope lies in the fact that God does not give us what we deserve.

To go back to the historical record of Moses, Pharaoh stands in history as an evidence that God's purpose will inescapably be delivered; His power unquestionably demonstrated; and who He is declared universally for all to see as well as hear. Don't ever forget that you can never play fast and loose with God. Pharaoh persisted in hardening his own heart against God long before God hardened it.

There is an often forgotten spiritual axiom here, that whatever we sow, that shall we also reap. God accedes to our desires to control our own lives and to dismiss His purposes wilfully by saying, "If that's the way you want it, then that's the way you can have it!" God does not give us up but He does give us over to our own devices. That alone explains and defines His dealings with Pharaoh – and, for that matter, the rest of us. So don't grumble and complain and protest when God chooses to have mercy on some and to harden the hearts of others. It is not that the promises of God have failed, but that the people of God have failed.

I know that this causes a significant and severe reaction from you! You may well be feeling: "This teaching removes the ground from beneath my feet! How does God quantify rebellion against Him; resistance to Him; and rejection of Him?" Be very careful when you want to give

God back-chat! You are in danger of wanting an argument and a debate rather than facing up to reality. Go down to the potter's house. The potter makes a beautiful vase for flowers or for a household decoration, but a plain, rough, ordinary dish for food. He decides!!! He has complete control of and authority over the clay – its shape is determined by what he has in mind and it will be fashioned accordingly. I so realise that this is offensive to you; that God has the right to manage the affairs and circumstances of your life.

Right at the heart of this attack, that God is unfair, lies a real ignorance of His character. God, by definition and nature, will never, never do anything that is unjust or unfair. God does what He does because He is what He is. His character determines His conduct. You see, God wants His Creation to know the reality of His anger and His power – hence the Pharaoh story! (Ten times God said to Pharaoh, "Let my people go!" And ten times Pharaoh said, "No!" to God).

God is saying "I chose you to demonstrate my power to the whole world!" Even with our limited understanding there is nothing unfair about that, is there? God has chosen to demonstrate His mercy, not because of human preference or performance, but because He chose to demonstrate His patience and His power by not giving – not only Jews but also non-Jews – what they deserve.

I want you to think carefully how God wanted to communicate the lavishness and limitlessness of His radiance and fullness towards those who were undeserving, and so He destined them for this purpose – and that gloriously means you and me whom he has called for this purpose. It is not a question of our race but of His grace (the sheer undeserved and unearned generosity and favour of His heart!). Oh, dear friends, go back to that tender and intrusive prophecy of Hosea where God says:

"I own those who have not known My Covenant promises to my people, Israel, simply because they have responded to my sheer undeserved generosity and favour; and I will embrace those who appear to have forfeited my love by their behaviour."

And again:

"Where it seems that you have been rejected, you will be accepted."

In a rather more terrifying way the prophet, Isaiah, spoke out of the heart of God all those years ago:

"Be warned, my people, Israel, though you have multiplied in number, not all of you will be in my final purposes because I am Judge as well as Saviour, and some of you have forfeited your destiny."

In the same way the prophet, Isaiah, said:

"Unless God Almighty had preserved a remnant from His people, Israel, our destiny would have been as comprehensive and complete in destruction as occurred at Sodom and Gomorrah."

You see, God's choices are not arbitrary, capricious, or irrational – they are because He has a purpose. The reason God chooses some Jews and not others is a double demonstration of His justice and His mercy to other people who do not even belong to the Jewish nation. What a wonderful message according to Hosea, "Not everyone outside of Israel will be lost". What a sombre message according to Isaiah, "Not everyone within Israel will be saved". Indeed, if God were simply just, the Jews would have vanished out of history altogether – if God had given them what they deserved!

So, what shall we make of all this? This is one of the most ironic things in all of human history – some of those who were not looking to get right with God, got right with God because they trusted implicitly in what He said and what he did; and some who desperately wanted to get right with God didn't get right with God because they thought they could get right with God by the way they lived and by the things they did. They couldn't get their heads round the fact that God had come out of eternity into history in the Person of the Messiah they had been expecting for so long, and His name was Jesus!

They failed to grasp that seven hundred years previously God told them, through the prophet Isaiah, that the very One who would bring stability and hope caused them to falter and fail because they did not recognise who Jesus really is. Oh, my dear kinsmen, there are none so blind as those who don't want to see. God had said so plainly and simply that Jesus – God come among men and women in human flesh; their Messiah – would never disappoint or betray anyone who not only believed ABOUT Him but believed IN Him.

∽CHAPTER 10∽

I cannot leave it there because the implication for me is far too personal and deep. From the fathomless depths of my being, with inarticulate longings before God, I cry out to Him that my kinsmen might find peace with Him in a precious and indestructible bond.

You see, my whole ancestry is Jewish, and I know how consumed Jews are to get right with God and bring Him pleasure. However, they have gone about it in the wrong way! They thought they could earn God's favour and get right with Him by the things they did rather than by the thing God did. They arrogantly believed that they knew better than God how to get right with Him so they substituted 'I'll do it my way!' in the place of 'He'll do it His way!'

Be absolutely convinced and utterly persuaded that Jesus – the Messiah – put an end to confining legalism and binding rule-keeping, and released us from practising religion and brought us into a personal relationship with Himself – a relationship of trust and reliance.

Previously I have spoken about divine sovereignty, but now I am speaking about human responsibility. Divine sovereignty emphasises that God chooses but human responsibility is also involved – and both are necessary! This is the really hard bit; that even if God's will is always the final factor, human responsibility remains a reality! God did not choose all the Jews, but then not all the Jews chose Gods way. How absurd does that sound? But, absurd or not, it is really true! The reason that some Jews are not in God's blessing, though they sought it, is due to God's choice and man's choice together.

Look at Jewish history as far back as Moses himself (recorded in the Book of Leviticus) to whom God spoke and said "No one will have to go up to God to bring the Law down to you, and no one will have to go down to the grave to ask, 'What does the Law say?'" You have the law now, so apply it! Back then God made it abundantly clear that if you want to get right with Him by keeping the rules and obeying the Law then that must always be by comprehensive obedience. It unquestionably and unalterably lays the responsibility on you.

However, to get right with God – God's way – is with your ears and not with your hands. It is both internal – it involves the heart – and external – it involves the lips. Our hope and salvation comes by what we believe and not how we behave. It is by our heartfelt words and not by our diligent works. It is by declaration not by deeds. It is centred on grace not on race. It is about Jesus not about Jewishness. It is about a confession that Jesus is who He claimed to be – Jehovah – and about a conviction that He lived, died, and conquered the grave. That is the only basis, hope, and security – a conviction that He is alive today – that we have been put right with God. It is not about what we do, but it is about what He has done.

Be absolutely assured that the Bible teaches that anyone – Jew or non-Jew – who relies upon, and is committed to Jesus will never be either disappointed or let down. It is so easy to seek the right God in the wrong way. Be assured – in spite of what you may have heard or wanted – God has no favourites! He is even-handed and wants to enrich and benefit all who will cry out to Him out of the poverty and pain of their humanity.

47

Long, long ago God declared that finding peace with Him depended on our awareness of our human helplessness and our despairing hopelessness and our heartfelt cry to Him to give us what we don't deserve, and to refrain from giving us what we do deserve.

Let's face it, you can't cry out to someone unless and until you believe that someone is alive. Equally, you cannot believe that that someone is alive unless you have heard conclusively and plainly that he is alive. What you hear can never be the uncertainty and hesitancy of someone's opinion, but a clear, authoritative message from heaven to earth that is not up for discussion but is the Good News of God. That's why it is so essential that a person like me comes to share this staggering and dramatic reality with you. Do you not realise that seven hundred years ago one of your own prophets – Isaiah – declared, "How wonderful and attractive are the messengers who come bringing good news to us!"

To this day, Jews read the prophecy of Isaiah but did not accept the Good News of which he spoke. It's not that all Jews haven't heard his Message, but not all Jews have heeded it! Do you really not realise that trust in and dependence on God comes through your ears, and that life-transforming reality comes from the lips and incarnate life of the Messiah, Jesus?

It is a simple fact of history that there is not a single Jew in any part of the world who has not heard the Good News of that Messiah declared and proclaimed. Everywhere the Jews have gone, the Good News has gone. Your problem, my fellow-kinsmen, is not that you need a hearing-aid; your problem is that you need a heeding-aid!!

I cannot repeat or over-emphasize my amazement that you remain in bewilderment and ignorance of all of this. Long ago, Moses sang a prophetic song in the presence and hearing of every Israeli so that Jews could hear God say:

"You made me jealous by going after other gods, so why should you be upset when I go after other people whom you consider to be foolish and

48

lacking not only in background but also in the godly traditions that are part of your culture."

It was also brave of the prophet, Isaiah, to declare:

"Non-Jews who had not been waiting for nor looking for the Messiah found Him in Jesus. This is the gut-wrenching truth that those non-Jews who have little or no knowledge of the Scriptures know Me because I have revealed myself in My Son, Jesus, the Messiah."

Again Isaiah said:

"You do not really know My heart. It is not that I am vindictive or punitive towards My People, Israel, for I have longed to embrace them as long as there was the light of day. But their proud hearts and stubborn wills prevented them from discovering and experiencing My warmth and welcome."

It is not the inflexibility of God's choice that is operating here but the intransigence of man's pride that says: 'I will do it my way!'

∼ CHAPTER 11 ∼

In the light of what I have written, I want to ask you a question: 'Have you come to the conclusion that God does not keep His promises, and has completely washed His hands of His people, Israel, and has no further interest in them? Nothing could be further from the truth! When God makes a promise, He keeps it. It is true that once I was a Jewish Jew and now I am a Christian Jew, but I am still a Jew.

As a Jew, you can trace my ancestry and you will find that it is impeccably Jewish both by lineage and by location. God always had the Jewish people in His heart for He had plans for them and through them, and that has never changed in spite of everything! God is not capricious and fickle. Read the history of our people and you will remember how one of our prophets, Elijah, was tormented and in pieces because of how things appeared. Circumstances had broken him into devastating bewilderment – godly messengers killed; holy meeting-with-God places desecrated and vandalised; personally abandoned; fearful of death. Where is God now in all of this, he wondered?

What about His people, Israel – obliterated and gone? Do you remember what God said? He said, "Elijah, you have jumped to the wrong conclusion. Many of my People have defected to immoral and idolatrous Baal worship, and have turned their backs on me, but 7,000 have remained faithful to Me in the face of pressures, persecutions, tensions, and problems because I have held them securely in My grip."

You see, this is a God-thing – their security lay not in their ability to hold on to God, but on His ability to hold on to them. This principle – this God-thing – continues, even as I am writing to you now; God has not given up on the Jewish nation, for out of the sheer, undeserved generosity and favour of His heart He is holding on to some of our kinsmen. Please, please notice that it is not because they have earned His favour or deserve His generosity, but because He refuses to give them what they really deserve. 120 Jews in a Jerusalem Upper Room; 3,000 Jews at the Jewish Celebration of Pentecost; 5,000 Jews on the day that two Jews – Peter and John – got arrested – all Jews responding by faith to the sheer, undeserved generosity of God's heart!

Don't you get it? What our kinsmen desired with all their hearts eluded them because many of them thought that the means to that end of getting right with God was by trying harder to please God, when, in fact, it was by trusting more in who He was and what He said. Check it out in the lives of Abraham, Isaac, Moses, Joshua, Caleb, Samson, Gideon, Barak. They got it!!! God held on to them and blessed them; used them; provided for them; spoke to them – even in the weakness of their humanity, because it was not down to them, it was up to Him.

Would you notice and take seriously another God-thing: when God notices people who will not heed this incredible Good News – that we can only be in God's good books by what we hear and not by what we do – He doesn't give us up, but He gives us over to do it our way until we get to the point where we cannot heed the Good News. It is a spiritual principle that God says: "If that's the way you want it, then that's the way you can have it!"

Long ago Moses and Isaiah declared:

"Muddled thinking; blinded eyes. Deafened ears that could not hear. Even now they walk in darkness; Light of truth they could not share."

King David, the prophet, declared the same thing:

"National feasts became their prison; Tripping, falling, sightless eyes. Punishment became their portion; Bearing burdens was their prize."

I keep on asking questions because I want you to give answers. I want you to notice that there are two kinds of falling – you can fall in such a way that you never get up again. However, that's not the way the Jews fell. Their fall was neither final nor fatal! The Commandments which were intended to be a manifestation that they were going to heaven became, for them, the means by which they got there. So trying was substituted for trusting, and so many stumbled and fell.

But I have been pointing out that God's rejection of the Jews was neither total in the past, nor is it fatal in the present. God is much bigger than our failures! God used their failure to bless non-Jews. The stark reality of non-Jews being enormously blessed and wonderfully rescued has caused Jews to consider the truth in a different light, and set up longings within them to possess by faith what they could not earn. Look at the consequences of all of this – universal enrichment for every culture; unimaginable blessing to non-Jews. It is inconceivable what indescribable and immeasurable impact and influence their closing in with God's offer will have.

51

I want you who are non-Jews to hear clearly what I am saying. From the very moment that I met the risen Jesus on the road to Damascus I have never doubted my calling. Strange as it may seem to you, and unbelievable as it is to me, God asked me to be a missionary to non-Jews. As I write to you now, I am pursuing my calling from God with all my heart and soul, anticipating eagerly that what I have to say to non-Jews will cause Jews (my own kith and kin) to become jealous as they realise what they have missed through teaching and tradition that led them astray.

My fervent hope is that some will turn around and find the reality of salvation in Jesus. Just think about this for a moment; if the consequence of their failure and folly is universal hope and healing, what will be the consequence of their faith and fulfilment through Jesus, their Messiah? The only way to speak of the magnificence of that would be the triumph and the extravagance of resurrection. It is not the branch that supports the root, but the root that supports the branch. If the root is right, then the branch is right.

I'm not a man of the soil; my background is urban; but I know that in normal horticultural terms the procedure is to graft the cultivated stock onto a wild stock so as to produce good fruit or flowers. However, with the olive tree it is different – the wild stock is grafted onto the cultivated stock. So, non-Jews, don't get too far ahead of yourselves. You are like wild olive branches, and you have been grafted into the cultivated olive tree root. It is from that root that you will get nourishment, support, and life. In a word, you are supported by Jewish roots. You have been grafted into Jewish stock.

Because Jewish branches were broken off and withered and died, you have been given the opportunity to be grafted into life. So, as you review the history of God's People, Israel, you will come to the conclusion that some of them died so that you could live. Be absolutely clear, however, that they died because they could not accept and respond to God's offer of life to them, undeserved and unearned – but you grasped the undeserved favour and generosity of God with both hands; a warm, responsive heart; and a committed and surrendered life.

Be very careful how you respond to all of this. You must learn to think about God; respond to God; approach God as the Hebrews did. You do not have any immunity against the severity and judgment of God. Be assured that as soon as you substitute your way for God's way, you are out in the cold, too – branches broken off and abandoned. That's what happened to the Jews, and it will happen to you too – God does not change!!

All of us want to dwell on God's kindness, but be aware, also, of God's judgment as well as His mercy; of His truth as well as His grace; of His light as well as His love. Assuredly, you have known God's kindness, but you will only continue to experience that kindness as you continue to trust rather than to try – depending on what he has done perfectly, fully, and finally and not on what you are able to do. Turn your back on that and you will know the severity of God – just like the Jews.

Just for the record, God is certainly not finished with the Jews – He has not washed His hands of them! What has been broken off can be grafted in again. If life, fragrance, and fruitfulness can come to uncultivated branches, like you non-Jews being grafted into a cultivated root, think what would happen when cultivated branches, which belonged to the cultivated root, are grafted into the olive tree to which they belong. Although God has called me, primarily, to bring Good News to non-Jews, my heart is singing with a message of hope and a future for my fellow-kinsmen if they will turn from doing life their way and begin to do it God's way.

I really want to dispel from your minds any misunderstanding of what is happening. This unfolding plan has always been in God's heart and amazingly He wants you, who trust and obey Him, to grasp it so that you will never be tempted to swagger at what seems to be a new deal. God is going to bring His People, Israel, back into the fullness of His blessings and purposes for them. Your future destiny is bound up with theirs. God has fixed the number of non-Jews He plans to save – however offensive and unacceptable that might be to you. Hope and a future burns brightly for the Jews as was prophetically promised to them seven hundred years ago:

"From the hill on which the Holy City stands, Your hope will come, embracing all the lands. Rebellion gone; deception turned aside; A new relationship upon a Saviour blessed; Sin dealt with; hope restored at last."

As far as the Good News, brought to us through the perfect work of Jesus, is concerned, the Jews appear to be hostile and so give you hope; but as far as God's purposes are concerned the Jews have always been promised a special place. As I have been saying so often to you, God always keeps His word. If God calls a non-Jew, it is always because of a sheer act of His not giving him what he deserves. If God calls a Jew, it is always because of a sheer act of His not giving Him what he deserves. Be completely convinced that if any of us is in the Family of God, it is because of God's mercy and not His justice, whether we are Jews or non-Jews.

We are all out of our depth when it comes to measuring God's wisdom and knowledge! His verdicts and conclusions baffle our most persistent attempts to grasp them. The way that He prescribes and the plans He has for us are beyond our ability to identify. His thoughts cannot be fully understood even with the most agile and perceptive human thinking. No one could ever hope to give our God good advice. No one could ever put God in his debt. Out of Him; from Him; and belonging to Him flows everything that there ever was and ever will be. To this God of ours be the splendour, the radiance, the fullness, and the completeness of all things in history and in eternity – Oh yes! Oh yes! Oh yes!

∼ CHAPTER 12 ∼

I realise that this has been quite a letter that I have written to you so far. I have stretched your minds and I have insisted on your having a clear and correct understanding of who God is; how God acts; and what God wants. He is a God who does not want to give anyone – Jew or non-Jew – what they deserve.

As a result of all that I have already written to you I want you to apply physically, visibly, and intentionally what you have understood to be true – your beliefs must always be demonstrated by your behaviour. Salvation must always lead to service; what He has done must have a response in what you must do; visible evidence must always follow invisible reality. What I am getting at is that the time has now come for you to do something in the light of what I have written.

The first thing to do is to worship God in Spirit and in truth. We are here as worshipers first and workers second. Be in no doubt that the work done by a worshiper will have eternity in it. The Hebrews were taught to bring a dead body to express their worship, but things are different now; you are to bring a living body – your body – and offer yourself to God completely, finally, and fully without reservations. You have been forgiven, cleansed, and made fit for Him to accept and use!

Although you are in Rome, don't do as the Romans do! Don't let the world squeeze you into its mould. The only way that you can avoid this is by having a new, radical, and revolutionized way of thinking. What your body does is conditioned by the way your mind thinks. Be sure, there are no short-cuts to guidance. These are the two steps which alone will enable you to know what God wants you to know – ONE, offering your body with every ability you have; every faculty you possess; every attitude you adopt; and every security you long for; and TWO, changing your mind from every pre-conceived idea; every prejudice; every natural, human response; and every traditional concept.

Laying your body and mind irrevocably before God may seem reckless and even dangerous, but be absolutely convinced that God's plans for you are without any negative, dark shadows; they are ultimately and inevitably attractive; and they are absolutely tailor-made to fit you!

What I want to say to you now, I only dare say it to you because I am a recipient of what I could never win, earn or gain. I want you to have a right attitude to yourself – never have a higher view of your ability, your capability, your position, your importance, or your effectiveness than is real. On the other hand, never put yourself down! Remember God made you; He redeemed you; He has filled you with His Holy Spirit.

Think deeply about all of this and try to get it right. Remember that Christian service is not only FOR people, it is WITH people. You cannot cooperate with others properly unless and until you consider and assess yourself properly! Look at your own body and how it works. If the different members of your body could talk they would never claim to have the same function, yet in their diversity there is unity and harmony. That is how the new Body of Christ on earth – the Church – works. Real effectiveness will always depend on radical and intrusive association with others.

Clearly, we have different gifts – not because we have either earned them or deserved them, but because of God's lavish generosity. So let's think about this – if a person's Gift is the supernatural ability to speak out what is on God's mind and heart by the inspiration of the Holy Spirit, then let him do that depending on God and trusting Him to speak into his mind and emotions. If a person's Gift is showing the love of Christ in doing things that need to be done, then let him do these practical things in an effective and creative way. If a person's Gift is explaining what has been proclaimed as the message of Christ, then let him do that diligently knowing that exhortation and proclamation and invitation often need explanation. If a person's Gift is affirmation and exhortation, then let him do that so that the discouraged and the downhearted are kept standing on their feet. If a person's Gift is meeting the poverty of others out of his plenty, then let him do that with prodigal generosity. If a person's Gift is being called to occupy a leading place, then let him do that with humility, authority, responsibility, and consistency. If a person's Gift is giving to others what they don't deserve, then let him forgive with gracious, warm-hearted kindliness and not with criticism, contempt, and a superior attitude.

56

Because of what God has done for you, you have a responsibility for others. Let me give you a check-list to help you develop your relationship with those who are bound up in the bundle of God's life with you.

To begin, make sure that you want the best, the most, and the highest for others whatever you might perceive that to be for them. Be sure that you have no hidden, personal agenda or ulterior motive in building a significant relationship with others. Realise that true love is always compatible with hatred – covet what is light, and hate what is darkness; long for what is fulfilling, and challenge what is frustrating; reach out to what is creative, and resist what is destructive. Remember always that the Church is not a Club or a society or an organisation – it is a family; so act accordingly!

The world struggles to get prestige and position and privilege for itself. That must never be your objective, for you are to promote others rather than yourself. Never go off the boil so far as the Holy Spirit is concerned, but let Him cascade over into the lives and circumstances of others as you focus on pleasing Jesus.

Face up to the fact that there are never hopeless situations, only people who have lost hope, and have become submerged in despair. A new day dawns for you when you realise that with God failure is never final! Don't give up too quickly or give in too soon when you feel the darkness is closing in on you and you sense difficulties could easily overwhelm you.

Never forget that God has lips as well as ears, so guard a consistent attitude deep within you of wanting to hear what God is saying and then making an obedient and unrestricted response. That, of course, will mean giving space and time in your life schedule to listen for God to speak to you. Be sensitive to those alongside you who call God 'Father' and care for them in practical ways. Never allow your home to become a 'closed shop'.

There will always be those around you who make life difficult for you; oppose you; damage you; and cause you heart-ache. Respond to them in a different spirit from that which causes them to attack you. Try to walk 'in the moccasins' of those around you; seeing life from their point of view.

Challenge friction and fractured relationships wherever they are found. Be aware that people can humiliate us, but only one person can humble you – you!! Be careful not to judge people by their occupation. Manual and menial work are both important to God. After all, His Son worked at a carpenter's bench and washed dirty feet when no one else was prepared to do that. So, don't wear airs and graces and look stupid!

Pay attention to the fact that to return evil for evil is how the beasts behave; to return good for good is how men and women behave; to return evil for good is how the devil behaves; but to return good for evil is how Jesus behaves – so copy Him! Remember it is not only important to do what is right, but it is also important to be seen to be doing what is right.

I realise that situations and circumstances can be difficult and complicated, but so far as you are concerned, always try to pour oil on troubled waters. When situations boil over and provoke you to act in retaliation, make a conscious decision, as a direct act of your will, to quell your anger and positively put the situation into God's hands to handle it in His way. He made a promise long ago, in Deuteronomy, that He was perfectly capable of handling such a situation without your help. Your responsibility is to bless those who are hostile to you, and not to curse them; to serve them and not to spurn them. That will have a far more significant effect than anything you could ever do. Never allow evil to dictate or dominate your life. Light is more powerful than darkness, and goodness is more effective and creative than badness.

∽ CHAPTER 13 ∽

Having dealt with life and relationships within the Church, I now want to turn to life and relationships within society. In other words, I want to deal with what it means to be a good citizen as well as a good Christian. Be in no doubt that part of being a 'living sacrifice' is willingness to submit to authority. This is a major issue and a key theme in all that I have written not only to you, but to many others under the control and direct inspiration of the Holy Spirit.

I have no authority to tell you what is the best government, but I have authority to tell you to accept the form of government that exists – for those in civil authority over us have been ordained by God regardless of what they think and what we think. The implication of this is enormous – to resist the government is to resist God!! The Christians attitude and response to the government is obedience, not resistance (unless that government is despising and dismissing God's laws and defaming Jesus Christ).

I realise that this is a radical and revolutionary thought and teaching to you, who live at the very seat of a government which is dictatorial and pagan. Be very careful how you receive and react to what I am writing to you lest you find yourself not only under civil but also under divine disapproval with all that that implies.

The first function of a government, in God's sight, is to control, restrain and punish those who do wrong and perpetuate evil. The government has been put there by God in the first place to demand justice not to dispense welfare. God ordained that evil should be restrained and punished by the State. The way to be free from uncertainty and apprehension, so far as the State is concerned, is to do what is right. By living that way, you have nothing to fear.

Please notice that the ability God has given the government is to use force. The sword is the instrument of justice, and it is neither a toy nor a meaningless symbol. Those who do wrong are right to be afraid, whether they are within the State (i.e. evil-doers) or outside the State (i.e. aggressors). There is a clear difference between the government official and you – he is there to restrain evil, if necessary, by force as a channel of God's anger; whereas you are there to promote good as a channel of God's sheer, undeserved generosity and favour. So submit to the civil authorities, not only out of fear of physical punishment, but so that you can demonstrate the goodness of God.

Because of all this, you have a responsibility to provide not only for Ministers in the Church, but also for Ministers of State so that they have the money by which they can live and the means whereby they can enable the State to do its job properly. Taxes are to be paid, and money to service State responsibilities must be given. Not only are you required to take the right action in this, but you are also required to have the right attitude to this. If the government is to do its job properly it must have your respect. A government which loses respect will lose all fear and so lose the ability to do what God put it there to do in the first place.

I want to continue to explore with you the responsibilities you have within society. If you enter into a contract you must honour it whether it is the money you owe; the promises you make; or the time you agree to be present and to work. Be very careful about contracting obligations you are unable to meet.

However, there is a debt you owe to everyone, and that will never come to an end. The constant debt you will have to the end of life's journey is to want the best, the most, and the highest for the people around you, whoever they are. The Commandments that God gave to Moses, and he gave to God's people, Israel, were given not to provide a way by which God's people could get to heaven, but to provide a framework for living for those who were already going there because of God's sheer, unearned, and undeserved favour.

For example, have respect for the sanctity of sex; have respect for the sanctity of life; and have respect for the sanctity of property. Love is not a vague thing but has substance and reality. Love can only exist when there is respect for these three things towards the people that you live amongst. Get a hold of the Ten Commandments in the Book of Exodus in the Jewish Torah and you will soon realise that the ten things commanded there can be summarized by loving God with all your heart, soul, mind and strength, and loving those around you as you want to love yourself. So, as far as the Commandments are concerned that does it!

The framework for this is the undoubted and straightforward reality that Jesus will make a personal, visible return into the arena of history and the affairs of mankind – it will mean His presence after His absence; the shining of His glory after His humiliation; and the unveiling of His majesty and power after the concealing of His lowly birth at Bethlehem. Don't put this on the back-burner to be considered when it might strike you more forcibly that it does now.

Obviously the moment of His return is more immanent than when you first became Christians. The darkness is beginning to recede and the first faint streaks of the dawning of a New Day are beginning to appear. So, deal with anything that is ungodly and ugly and unacceptable and pursue the protective shield of righteousness and godliness. Anti-social behaviour to people around us springs from unresolved and ungodly problems within us. Live in such a way that secret and hidden shame is banished. Deal with the noisy, excited, and uncontrolled demand for your own physical and sexual satisfaction that neglects and disregards others so as to achieve what you perceive to be happiness.

Control your intake of alcohol whereby you become a nuisance to others and a danger to yourself. Refuse to abase and soil your God-given sexuality. Be careful about the exhibitionism which has lost all sense of shame and decency and parades evil publicly. Get a grip of any tendency to disagree with anyone about everything. Be very wary of the green-eyed monster that is never content with what it has, and constantly covets what others have.

Instead of all that distasteful stuff allow Jesus to take the driving-seat of your life; reign as Lord in your heart; and become all that He always wanted to be in you and through you and for you. Make a conscious effort to change your mind-set, so that good would take the place of evil; light the place of darkness; and God-honouring living rather than self-pleasing life.

∽CHAPTER 14∽

Be aware that there are other things – very different from those things that I have been writing about – that can often be a hindrance to the development and demonstration of your Christian lives. You see, among you there are those who come out of very different backgrounds, traditions, and experiences of life – both Jews and non-Jews. Be careful that you do not jump to conclusions about them on the basis of what they do or don't do.

One person's understanding of his diet is that he is free to eat and drink anything because God has created all that he eats and drinks in the first place, before men and women associated meat with idolatry and so contaminated it. Another person who hasn't yet grasped the radical and totally transformed life in Christ still has scruples about eating meat because of its former association with idolatry. The person who has the firmer grasp of what it really means to be a Christian and has fewer rules and regulations governing his behaviour must be careful not to regard who has not come into this radical freedom in Christ as inferior.

By the same token the person who still maintains certain taboos and prohibitions to govern his behaviour must be careful not to become censorious and judgmental towards the person who now lives free from them. Diet must never determine devotion. Be aware that the determining factor is not what YOU think; it is what GOD thinks that really matters. Realise that you are not another person's master. It is to God that he, as well as you, is responsible. Each of you does what he does because he wants to please God. So welcome each other as brothers, and not because his behaviour is like yours! At the end of the day God is his judge, not you!

The same principal is applied to days and festivals. May I encourage you to think clearly and come to conclusions and convictions that are not based on human customs and conventional thinking, but are based on answering the question: 'What will honour the Lord?' So think clearly; consult other mature Christians; and, above all, let your answer to that question govern your behaviour.

You see, living or dying we are to honour the Lord and live in the glorious reality of His salvation. If you start there and think things through from there – whatever conclusion you come to needs to be respected even when some others do not share it. It is not what goes into your mouth that makes you unclean, but what goes on in your mind that soils you.

My word to you who have really grasped what it means to be free in Christ and enjoy that liberty from taboos of meat and drink and Sabbath days and festivals; no longer living under the law but in the joy of the lavish generosity of God's heart and favour; ruled, not from the outside but from the inside, by the guidance and direction of the Holy Spirit; to be tender and respectful with those who still wrestle and struggle with these issues in order to honour God. Those thought to be weaker in their understanding of the Faith are not accountable to those thought to be stronger in their understanding of the Faith. All of us, one day, as Christians, will give an account to God for what we have done with our Christian lives since we became Christians.

Seven centuries ago God spoke out of eternity into history of His unchangeable authority and declared: "All men, everywhere, will submit and surrender to Me not only with their lips but also with their lives." Be absolutely sure, each one of us, individually and personally, will give an answer to God for the way we have lived and behaved, remembering that our liberty through Jesus will never become either licence or lax.

To sum all this up, stop pointing the finger at others in your fellowship. Instead of doing that, make sure that you do not make life even more difficult than it already is for anyone. I want you to know that though I am living in the lavish flood-tide of the freedom with which the Lord Jesus has set me free from ritual and conventional prohibitions, I will not ride rough-shod over the scruples of others. I will honour and respect their position, for my first consideration will be to love them as my brothers and sisters in Christ.

If I cause them stress, anxiety and confusion by exercising my freedom, then I am no longer showing my love to them. Inconsiderately and thoughtlessly flaunting and boasting of my freedom in Christ can so easily remove life from one for whom the Messiah, Jesus, gave His life. Be very careful that what is undoubtedly good for you is not spoken of as bad by someone else. Stop arguing about food, drink, and observances and start emphasizing the really important things in the Christian life.

The really important things are learning to be like Jesus; living in unity, harmony, and fellowship with others; and having a praising heart without being critical, condemnatory, and censorious. To live this way you will need to be filled and flooded by the Holy Spirit. He will enable you to do anything not prohibited in Scripture; but He will also fill you with such love for your brother Christian that your freedom will always be limited by your consideration of him. All things may well be lawful for you, but be sensitive to the fact that not all things are always expedient. Any disciple of the Messiah, Jesus, who lives and behaves this way will bring pleasure to the heart of God and appreciation and endorsement from those among whom he lives.

In the light of all of this, you need to recognise again that you are here to bring harmony and a sense of well-being to others, and to contribute to building one another up to become strong and resilient in the Faith. Get things into perspective – do not jeopardize what God is doing because of what you are eating. A Christian is free to do anything not prohibited in Scripture – and to thank God for everything he has made and honour Him by enjoying His creation. But a Christian who says he will do what he believes to be right without consideration of anyone is wrong.

You may feel personally, and others may say openly, that this is inconsistent, hypocritical, and compromising, but do not listen to these internal and external voices for this is a matter that is settled in the secret place where only God is heard to speak. There is real happiness in restricting your personal freedom because of your concern about how it would affect others. In these circumstances, it will really help you to realise that your brother who has scruples is in that position because he, too, wants to honour and please God, and this is the way that he expresses his devotion.

Please realise that this person who is weaker in the Faith and has an over-scrupulous conscience may disregard, disobey, and silence his conscience for a whole variety of reasons. Please see that for him that is dangerous and disastrous, because to defy his conscience is sin if he believes a thing to be wrong and goes ahead and does it. A neutral thing becomes the right thing only when it is done out of the real, reasoned conviction that it is right.

This is no trivial or superficial matter. There is a principle that is clearly defined in Scripture that anything that does not find its origin and ultimately its expression as a result of faith is sin! I solemnly lay this whole matter of principle before you that you might use your freedom in Christ not to indulge as well as to indulge.

CHAPTER 15

In the light of all that I have written my concern is that there would be no unnecessary fragmentation and division among you, crippling the family of God. Fundamentally, we are not here to do or say what suits us best. Those of you who are robust in the Faith must not focus on what you are free to do but rather be considerate, sensitive, and kind towards those who feel they must restrict themselves because of their scruples and convictions. My concern is not that you would simply submit to what others want – and so try to please everybody – but that you would do and say what others need.

You see, a Christian satisfies neither his own pleasure nor his brother's pleasure but is concerned and driven by what will strengthen, develop, and encourage his brother's resilience in the Faith. Undoubtedly, to live this way will land you in trouble – criticised as naïve; condemned as unrealistic; confronted as being dishonest and inconsistent. Aiming to build and strengthen others in the Faith rather than affirming our own position is tricky and challenging. However, we have a perfect role model because God-made-flesh in Jesus was criticised, condemned, and ultimately crucified, because he didn't do what people wanted but He did what people needed.

The cry of my heart is that you would be dependable and stand firm when frustration, failure, and discouragement stare you in the face. You not only have the example of the Messiah, Jesus, but you have the Scriptures of the Torah to inspire and assure you that to live this way among God's people is effective and owned by God. So stand firm and tough it out when you are misrepresented and misunderstood so that you can face the future with your eyes shining with optimism and anticipation.

Let the Messiah, Jesus Himself, be your template for living in relationship with others in the family of God so that unity would be preserved. This is one of the reasons why Jesus came – to show us clearly what God is like; what God does; and what God wants. Living in harmony with one heart and voice is not simply for our benefit, but for God's blessing. It is so easy to have a private view of worship even in public, but God is looking for public devotion expressed in corporate worship.

You must be aware that the deepest division human history was to witness, is that between Jew and non-Jew. This is exactly what you struggle with.

Your church was originally comprised of Jews only; then non-Jews joined you. Persecution banished Jews from your great city and your church became comprised of non-Jews only. Years later the Jews returned and now you are a complete mixture of non-Jews and Jews.

Please realise the depth and strength of what is going on among you – it is deep-seated and generational. You think it is about days and diet – but it is far deeper than that. So, say to each other with warmth, integrity, and real conviction, "I really value you as my brother/sister!!" Remember how unlikely and unlovely you were when the Messiah, Jesus, received you under His rule and authority into His Kingdom. You non-Jews need to remember that Jesus was a Jew sent to fulfil all that the Law was and the Prophets said. You Jews need to remember that Jesus came to save non-Jews and refused to give them what they deserved.

God never called a non-Jew to become a Jew, nor a Jew to forfeit his racial inheritance and become a non-Jew. He called all of you to repent of sin; recognise and receive His Son, Jesus, as Lord and Saviour; and be immersed, saturated, and released in His Holy Spirit. So Jews need to welcome non-Jews and non-Jews need to welcome Jews. Those of you who are Jews should have known that it was always God's intention, from the very beginning, that non-Jews would be part of God's whole purpose for His world so that He might be seen, with wonder and worship, to be a God who gives us what we don't deserve.

King David of Israel was certainly aware of the place of non-Jews in God's unfolding plan as he bursts out in song about that very thing in the Book of Psalms. Moses, too, in one of the Books written for Jews, called Deuteronomy, includes non-Jews in the song of gratitude and joy for God's dealing with Jews in gracious mercy, rather than deserved justice. Also, that great Jewish prophet, Isaiah, seven hundred years before God's Anointed One, Jesus, came saw non-Jews as well as Jews included in God's astounding and incredible master-plan.

I am calling you to get a grip of reality and stop focusing on the past, with its often unhelpful influences, and start anticipating all that God wants to lead you into in His future and eternal purposes which are radiant and resplendent with limitless possibilities. Allow the Holy Spirit to release unhindered well-being, exuberant living, and unrestricted hope into you and among you so that historical, racial, and traditional animosities and prejudices between Jew and non-Jew may disappear in the flood-tide of His undeserved and unfettered favour and generosity.

So far as I am concerned, fellow-members of the new Body of Christ on earth, the Church, there is no shadow of doubt in my mind and heart that you are equipped with virtue at every point – not only strong and committed, but generous and kind at the same time; well-versed in what we, as Christians, believe and hold dear; and well able to impart those beliefs and attitudes to those to whom you relate.

I realise that I have written to you without any fear or favour about quite a number of contentious issues so that the impact on you would be deep and lasting. I have done so, not because I feel better informed or superior to you, but because of my undeserved Calling from God to be a servant of God's Anointed One, Jesus, with a particular focus on non-Jews to offer not a dead animal but their living bodies to God by sharing the Good News of God's unearned and extravagant favour to them, enabling them to be pure and holy in His sight because of what He has done by His Holy Spirit.

I am unburdening my heart to you as I try to express the depth, the intensity, and the sense of privilege I feel as I recognise that all that I have done, and continue to do, is an expression of my new life in Christ Jesus, fulfilling the Calling of God on my life. You see, there is absolutely nothing I can say without wanting you to understand my personal helplessness and utter impotence apart from the reality of the risen, reigning Lord Jesus Christ, living His life in and through me as I fulfil my God-given responsibility in encouraging and facilitating non-Jews to surrender their lives to God in life-transforming obedience.

I have done this by declaring clearly with my lips the life-transforming Good News of God and demonstrating consistently with my life what it really means to be a Christian – living a naturally supernatural life in the power of the Holy Spirit so that things astonishingly occur which are utterly beyond human explanation, and can only be attributed to God. By living this way in word and deed I am convinced I have proclaimed and unveiled this glorious Good News of God from Jerusalem to Illyricum wherever I have gone.

The thing that has driven me through these years has become a burning desire and limitless yearning to make sure that this Good News, centred on the Anointed One, Jesus, would be grasped and fully understood by those who had never heard or even dreamed of such staggering truth before. Virgin territory – so far as the Good news of God is concerned – has always magnetized me. When I think about it I ask myself the question: 'Why should there be those who have the opportunity to hear this Good News twice when there are so many who have never heard it even once?'

More than seven hundred years ago one of the most distinguished of the Old Testament foretold that the day would come when those who were blind to the truth would see it, and those who were deaf to eternal hope and life-transforming salvation, would hear about it and understand it.

A full diary and a crowded programme has meant that I have been unable to meet up with you. However, I am convinced that I have done what was required of me in these geographical areas and so a long-cherished desire to meet you becomes a possibility, as I continue my journey through Europe to Spain. On this trip I so look forward to being with you and to have you affirm, encourage, and help me, practically, as I continue on my onward journey – but only after we have enjoyed and experienced some undistracted quality time together.

In the meantime I am making my way to Jerusalem where I intend to bring hope and encouragement to the poverty-stricken and persecuted church members there. The church members in Macedonia and Achaia have learned a fundamental principle of our Message that giving far and away outstrips the blessing of receiving. As a consequence they wanted to release some of their resources to bless their brothers and sisters in Jerusalem. They did not give me their gifts to take to the Jerusalem Church reluctantly or grudgingly but gladly and generously because of an inner desire and not because of some outward legalistic requirement. It was this inner constraint that made it an obligation for them and not an option.

You see, through the Jews the non-Jews have been gloriously enriched far beyond any kind of material blessing, and so the non-Jews have this deep inner constraint to encourage and bless the Jews at this time in their practical needs. This is what I am engaged in at the moment, and I know you will understand that I need to complete this task before I start out on my journey to that hub of vibrant civilization – Spain.

When I make that journey I will include you in my itinerary. Because you have been so much in my thoughts and prayers I know that when, at last, we meet the lavish and abundant overflow of God's sheer, undeserved favour and generosity through the Anointed One of God, Jesus, will cascade over into your lives.

I am so aware that this visit to Jerusalem will not be easy and so I wanted to ask you to pray for me using the triune Name of the Father, the Son, and the Holy Spirit. This is not a casual or courtesy request but it is the agonising cry of my heart. I not only will face danger from unbelievers in Judea, but I know I will encounter difficulties from believers in Jerusalem, because the gift I carry comes to Jews from non-Jews.

You know, as I do, that it is more blessed to give than to receive, but it is so hard for us, as human beings, to embrace that reality. On the other hand it is so often harder to receive than to give because of our proud and stubbornly independent spirit. How often we need to learn that the grace of giving needs to be met by the grace of receiving. But added to all that complicated behaviour and reaction is the fact that non-Jews are giving to Jews – so there are racial barriers added to social, personal, and psychological barriers.

Please pray for me that when I, at last, come to you I might come with a testimony of spiritual victory in Jerusalem and together we might experience the full, undiluted favour of God. May the God who is and who wants to bestow His well-being on you be with you until we meet together.

O God, please let it be so!

∼CHAPTER 16∼

When Phoebe delivers this letter to you, give her the warmest possible welcome. She has such a giving, servant heart which reaches out in concern and compassion for others, so that the whole Christian Family at Cenchreae has been immeasurably enriched by her presence and ministry. Don't let her feel that she is a stranger among you but take her quickly into your hearts like the true Family of God wherever it is found. I have no idea what needs she might have by the time she gets to you, but take the initiative and bless her practically. She certainly has never been slow to respond to the needs of others and I, too, have benefitted from her care and thoughtfulness.

Please give my very best wishes to Priscilla and Aquila, my precious companions in so many situations. If you don't already know, they faced life-threatening antagonism because of rampant anti-semitism in the Roman Empire. For the sake of God's people they have lived a nomadic and unsettled life – in Rome, Corinth, Ephesus, then back in Rome, and now finally in Ephesus. Wherever they were they provided hospitality, care, compassion, and often instruction in Kingdom truth in their home. No wonder non-Jews who became Christians, as well as myself, appreciated them for so much that they unhesitatingly did.

Greet Epaenetus for me. I feel so close to him. He brought so much encouragement to me when he was the first in the Province of Asia to respond to the Good News of God personally.

Greet Mary who has been unstinting in the use of her time and energy to make things happen among you.

Greet Andronicus and Junias, who are not only related to me but have also suffered with me. How tireless they have been as messengers of the Good News of Jesus. Did you know that they go right back to the time of the martyr, Stephen, who had such an influence on my life. They actually experienced new life in Jesus before I did.

Greet Ampliatus who from such lowly beginnings became such a key player in the life of the Church. I so value him!

Greet Urbanus, Stachys, and Apelles – all of them tried, tested, and not found wanting in their friendship, service, and ministry.

Greet the family relations, servants, and slaves of Aristobulus. What an influence that little community has been!

Greet another relation of mine, Herodion.

Greet those who became Christians as they served Narcissus. God alone knows their influence at the Imperial Court.

Greet Tryphaema and Tryphosa who, although their names may mean 'dainty' and 'delicate', have worked like Trojans among you to the point of absolute exhaustion.

Greet Rufus, that man with such a choice spirit and well-known saintliness in your church. How can I ever express the depth of my gratitude not only to him but also to his mother for her kindness and tenderness towards me?

How could I ever forget Asyncritus, Phlegion, Hermes, Patrobas, Hermas, Philologus, Julia, Nereus and his sister (what was her name?), and Olympas.

Please greet them with a whole host of others whose names I cannot even remember. Greet them appropriately and personally.

I speak for all the Churches in sending my very warmest greetings.

I should have finished this letter, but there are still things I want to write to you. I cannot tell you how strongly I feel about warning you against people who either are already among you or will come among you who want to cause dissension and disturb and even destroy your peace. There are others who will put hindrances in your way and make it so much harder for you to live the Jesus' life. They want to undermine, dilute, and confuse what you have been taught. Have nothing to do with them even when that might seem rude to you. You see, in spite of the façade of pious words and a religious attitude they do not honour our Lord Jesus Christ.

The truth is that they are attempting to satisfy deep needs within themselves. Their words are appealing and their attitude is beguiling, but they will lead you astray not by direct attack but by subtlety and plausible ideas. Your submission and surrender to the Lordship of Jesus is talked about everywhere and so I am confident you will not succumb to their influence. I want you to know how proud I am of you, and for that reason I am keen to make sure you distinguish the good from the bad; the pure from the corrupt; and the truth from the lie.

Be absolutely assured that the God of peace is not the God of evasion and lethargy, but the God of action and victory. God's peace comes not by submitting to the devil's ploys, but by overcoming and destroying them. The yearning of my heart is that you will enter into the sheer, unearned, and undeserved generosity and favour of our Lord Jesus.

I am not alone in wishing God's love and blessings on you – Timothy, Lucius, Jason, and Sosipater join me in this.

I, Tersius, have carefully recorded all that Paul wanted to share with you, but I, personally, wanted to be associated with all those others who wanted to greet you as members of God's family.

Gaius joins me, too, in sending his greetings – he not only has opened his heart to us but also his home.

Erastus, who carries significant responsibility in our community, and Quartus (such a dear brother!) also send their greetings.

Finally, I want to honour God who alone can enable you to stand firmly and securely against the shocks of the world and the assaults of temptation by His incredible power to sustain you, even when life is at its worst and circumstances at their most threatening. This Good News from God, who is its source, made visible and unmistakably real by Jesus Christ, has been transmitted by a whole variety of human beings whom God commanded to share His truth out of eternity into history, so that all men and women everywhere – both Jews and non-Jews – might come to know Him and respond to Him. Oh, it is to this God – with no boundaries to His knowledge; His presence; and His power; who is comprehensively complete – that I want to ascribe glory because of who Jesus is and what Jesus has done.

AMEN

THE GOD-LIFE
AND ITS FREEDOM

Paul's Letter to the

Galatians

Paul's Letter to the

GALATIANS

∾ CHAPTER 1 ∾

T HIS LETTER IS FROM PAUL who has been called and commissioned by God. Please forgive me for establishing my credentials right at the very beginning! I am doing this not because of personal vanity or as a result of irritation with those who denigrate and then dismiss my calling by the risen Christ but because I don't want you to discredit or distort the message I delivered to you through uncertainty about my authority, my integrity or my authenticity.

My appointment to be a man chosen and sent out by God did not come from the agreement of any human agency, nor was I authorized to be Christ's representative to the Gentiles by godly leadership, but I am who I am and I do what I do as a result of my direct, dramatic and life-transforming encounter with the Lord Jesus Christ on the Damascus Road – gloriously resurrected from death to life by the only One who could possibly do this, God the eternal Father.

This is not a subjective, proud aberration of an arrogant mind, because other Christians right here among us have begun living in the wonder and reality of this message of freedom; have accepted my authority and totally affirm the thrilling truth I am sharing with you now.

You met me when I was involved in my first missionary journey and you responded to the Good News of God in Christ which I brought you there in the province of Galatia- in towns like Iconium, Lystra, and Derbe. It is because of the reality that I know you experienced then that I am writing to you now for fear that you will be beguiled and persuaded that full salvation requires more than is offered and made gloriously possible in Christ alone.

May you be daily aware of the lavish, undeserved generosity and indescribable well-being that goes on coming to you from God our Father and His Messiah and our Master, Jesus. You certainly know that this same Jesus withheld nothing that He had or anything that He was in order to release us – body, soul, and spirit – from being captivated and overwhelmed by the selfish values and inherent destructiveness of this world into the freedom, joy, and ultimate reality of the purposes of God, to whom we ascribe radiant fullness and brilliant perfection without limit, in time or in eternity. May that ever be so for you all!

I want you to know that I am absolutely flabbergasted and completely dumbfounded that in such a short time you have transferred your allegiance from the Messiah who met your darkness with His light; your poverty with His riches; your pain with His peace; and your despair with His hope; and have changed the Good News of God's Master-plan which I brought to you into bad news. You have preferred to get involved in what you still have to do, instead of trusting in what God has already done for you so perfectly and completely.

I do not blame you totally, for I know that there are those who followed me, and are now among you, who have muddled and upset you by turning the Good News of God's Master-plan completely upside down and have corrupted the thrilling, liberating truth that I declared to you. However, you must take personal responsibility for whether you depend on Christ, who died for you and now lives in you, and then let your faith in His risen life demonstrate itself in goodness or build your goodness on your own efforts and then hope that you have done well enough.

I cannot speak strongly enough against any human or spiritual being who tampers with God's Good News, which we so clearly and so simply declared to you so that it becomes a gross perversion of the truth – let him be everlastingly damned to hell. In case you did not get it the first time I said it, I want to say it to you again that you serve the Church best by damning those who preach a false message contrary to God's amazing and extravagant grace.

There was a day when I was a high-flier in Judaism and I certainly coveted and courted the favour, admiration and approval of those around me. But those days are forever gone and now I live only to please God alone. Here I stand uncompromising in my determination to declare fundamental truth and to resist very persuasive human error. In this way alone can I be faithful to the Messiah whom I honour and serve.

There are those who want to undermine me and in doing so dismiss the message that I preach as inaccurate, untrustworthy, and subversive. I am so concerned that you would grasp that what I declared to you was neither the result of fanciful invention nor human tradition but was the consequence of divine revelation.

What I have shared with you was neither communicated to me by any human messenger, nor explained to me by any human teacher, but is the result of that dramatic, direct encounter which I had on the Damascus Road with Jesus, the Messiah. He so clearly showed me that we will never earn God's favour by trying to be good; that religion is gone forever and relationship with Him alone will make His favour real – achieving needs to be replaced by believing and trying needs to be replaced with trusting.

You already know about my past – how fanatically and frantically I tried to please God by what I did. I put all my energy into fervour but had very little concept of faith. During these days I not only shamefully and shamelessly tried to damage the people who trusted in Jesus Christ alone, to bring them into a new and right relationship with God, but I wanted to eliminate and destroy them.

Although still comparatively young I was totally captivated, both genetically and racially, by Judaism and demonstrated that commitment in the theology that I embraced and the rituals I performed. I was absolutely determined that Judaism would be the grave of Christianity and not its cradle. Little did I know that when God took centre stage, rather than me, things would radically change. Beyond Calvary with its darkness, its shadows, and its anguish; beyond Bethlehem with its angelic cradle song; beyond Sinai with its thunder-toned pronouncements of the Law; beyond Eden with its sinless symphony of physical beauty and moral purity; beyond Creation with its wonder-chorus when the morning stars sang together; there was God – infinite and eternal.

This God knew me before my mother did. It was this God who chose me before I was conceived let alone born. It was this God who called me in the midst of the years and commissioned me as His ambassador to the Gentiles. There was not, and still is not, the slightest reason to explain why He did this. It was all totally the result of the extravagant generosity of His heart, that He confronted me so powerfully and painfully with His Son, Jesus.

This was so intrusively real that I did not need to ask anyone's opinion or seek anyone's affirmation. Instead, I went into the desert for three years to receive what God wanted to give, and to allow Him to do all He needed to do in me, before I went back to the place of my first encounter with Jesus.

I realised during my three years in Arabia that I needed to face my past – that is why I went first of all to Damascus where I had been an object of fear. After that I was aware that I needed to go back to Jerusalem where I had become an object of faithlessness – a turn-coat to all those who held Judaism so dear.

I knew, too, that the spearhead and undoubted leader of the Early Church, Peter, was there and I wanted to visit him with the sole purpose of getting to know him. Time was short but the days we spent together were so significant. I swear that I was not in contact with any other of the Master's men, apart from James, who had grown up with Jesus in the Nazareth home and now played such a key role in the Jerusalem church.

I had one other place that I needed to visit – the place where I had been brought up; gone to school; and was known better than anywhere else – Tarsus, in the Syrian and Cilician region. Undoubtedly they would know that I had seriously gone off the rails, so far as they were concerned, and turned my back on what I had formerly declared and passionately believed to be true. Please credit me with integrity in the midst of all of this so that what I share with you is clearly seen to be the honest truth.

I was a total stranger to the Christian communities in Judea. All they had to go on was a nameless statement that the man who had been their personal antagonist was now their faithful apologist, wherever he went – declaring and defending the good news of God's Master-plan in Jesus that he had spent such a long time despising and debunking. The stunning thing about all this is that they totally believed what they heard because they saw God magnificently at work, changing a human being from bondage to blessing; from confusion to certainty; and from being a stumbling block to Jesus, the Messiah, into being a building block in His hands – what forgiveness; what grace; what humility!!

∼ CHAPTER 2 ∼

It is now seventeen years ago since I encountered the risen Jesus in that dramatic, dynamic, life-transforming event on the road to Damascus.

Everything has been fundamentally and profoundly different ever since. I still had inner struggles with my humanity – and maybe even demonic interference – trying to create doubt and uncertainty within me that I might just have got it badly wrong. I realised I needed re-assurance.

In the reality of this God spoke very clearly to me telling me to go back to Jerusalem. This time I was not to go alone but to take that trusted father-figure, Barnabas (with his well-known Jewish background), and that wild-card, Titus (with his well-known Gentile background), with me. I went to pour out my heart over my convictions and concerns about God's Master-plan in Jesus not only for Jews but for non-Jews too. I wanted to share openly, with no reservations, so I did so privately with those who seemed to carry responsibility. I was so sure, yet I felt I needed human sounding-boards to affirm and confirm what I was declaring with such confidence.

I was so wonderfully encouraged by the whole-hearted welcome that Titus – the non-Jew – received from the Christian brothers. This impressed me so much because some, who claimed to be Christians in name but were Jews in reality, had breached our privacy so they could gather whatever material they could about our release from religious rules and regulations and tried to put pressure on us to return to binding religious observances. But we did not budge and gave them no quarter so that vibrant relationship might never triumph over dead-hand religion and good advice might always be replaced with good news. Only then could we maintain our integrity and share confidently with you without any shadow of doubt or hypocrisy.

I said to you that I opened my heart to those who appeared to be high-profile, well-known, recognised leaders, not to impress you or to gain authority and authenticity for what I know is true, but simply to tell it like it is. The days are gone for me when I wanted to look good and curry favour with anyone. My days are dominated now by a determination to know and then do what pleases God – and I saw and heard that in His Son, Jesus, when He met me all these years ago so intrusively.

I really want you to know that I am not dependent on human agencies or the affirmation of people. Quite the reverse was the reality, for instead of being impressed by them they were impressed by the ring of truth which they saw in me. They were left in no doubt whatsoever that I had been God-called and Christ-commissioned to declare the good news of God's Master-plan in Jesus to non-Jews, in exactly the same way that Peter had been called and commissioned to liberate the Jews with that same Message. It was similar yet different but different yet similar.

God is so very much bigger than our background, our prejudices, our customs, our traditions, and our ideas. The staggering reality is that the life-transforming Good News that God gave me independently, He had also given to those solid and trusted apostles who had walked with and talked to our Master, Jesus, and had witnessed His devastating yet history-changing death; His triumphant resurrection; and His glorious ascension to the throne-room of the universe.

It was because of this that James, Peter, and John gave Barnabas and me such a hearty welcome without any reservations. They recognised that I, too, was the recipient of the sheer, undeserved generosity of the heart of God. They affirmed and encouraged my calling by God to non-Jews as they rejoiced in their God-validated calling to Jews. The one thing which concerned them was that somehow we would no longer have that passion – so central to Judaism and the heart of God – for the voiceless, the disadvantaged, and the deprived. I assured them that they need not worry since I know that only second to His hatred of idolatry is God's deep compassion for the poor.

You must realise how shocked and angry I was over Peter's behaviour in Antioch. You no doubt know that Antioch is very different from Jerusalem. You will also know that Antioch is the place where the followers of Christ were called Christians for the first time. Until now everyone believed that

Christians were simply a Jewish sect. It was generally understood that they differed from the Jews only in that they believed that the Messiah had come in contrast to the Jews who believed that the Messiah had not yet come. It was because of this serious misunderstanding I had to say to Peter publicly and painfully, "You are wrong! You stand condemned! You are a hypocrite! You are causing confusion because Christianity and Judaism are completely incompatible – they can never mix!

In the early days in Antioch Peter was content to eat food that was not kosher. Then visitors from Jerusalem arrived with their strong Jewish inheritance and convictions and Peter reverted to type – an innate fear of what people might think of him, say about him, or do to him. His powerful influence affected the others around him who had a similar background and before we knew where we were we had a facing-both-ways group; a foot-in-both-camps group; a lets-do-it-the-old-way group all rolled into one to contend with. So plausible did it all seem that even dear Barnabas was beguiled by this group and joined them.

When it dawned on me what was happening I could not remain silent for this was no trivial matter. There comes a time when basic, crucial, fundamental issues are at stake that truth is more important than unity. This was not a conflict between two religious systems – this was a life or death; a heaven or hell issue. Anything which jeopardises the Good News of God's sheer, undeserved generosity must be courageously challenged and directly confronted.

This is why I went public in confronting Peter. I said to him, "You are pandering to the man in the street with the delusion that somehow he can earn God's favour by his own efforts and consequently get to heaven because of his own achievements. This is the confusion you are causing by doing what you are doing and saying what you are saying. You have already discovered freedom from observing and practicing religious rules and regulations and now you are insisting that non-Jews must observe and practice these same religious observances, that you have discovered and demonstrated are worthless in securing a vibrant, personal relationship with God. Come on, Peter, get a grip!"

You and I know perfectly well, because of our life-time traditions, that religious practices never secured peace with God for any of us. We know, with our background, that the only way that can happen is not by trying harder but rather by trusting completely in the perfect life and the accepted death of Jesus, the Messiah. This is not a dead theological principle but a living, vibrant, personal experience that has set us free, given us hope, and enriched our living beyond compare. It is because our theology is reality in our living, that we are so sure that this is the one and only way for everyone without exception.

I am so aware of the huge dangers inherent in this glorious good news of God's Master-plan in His Son, Jesus. For instance, there are those who would try to argue that if trusting in Jesus is all you need to be put right with God then we can sin to our heart's content. But trusting in Jesus alone for salvation is not a licence to sin and a carte-blanche to do wrong. Oh, Peter, you have allowed people by their logic to over-ride your experience of Christ and over-rule the teaching of Scripture. Be assured, Jesus never lowered standards.

In taking us away from depending on the Commandments He was not dragging us lower but lifting us higher. I could never go back from being a fulfilled and completed Jew because of, and in the Messiah, Jesus, to being crushed by the legalistic demands of Judaism. Peter, you feel guilty because you left the Commandments, but I would feel guilty if I went back to them, because you don't become a law-breaker by leaving the Commandments behind. You become a law-breaker by going back to them knowing that all you will prove is that you are unable to fulfil them.

It really is a killing business to live an absolutely and comprehensively good life. No one tried harder than me – and I think I got ahead of most – but it killed me! Literally, the Law brought me to a dead end. I realised the Law was not going to help me so I finished with the futility of trying and entered into the incredible freedom of trusting in the perfect, completed, finished work of Jesus on the Cross to save me. You see when you have been to the place of death you are in the place of possible resurrection.

That is what happened to me – I exchanged dead religion for a living relationship with Jesus Christ, enabling me now to live the God-life. The old racially-pure, morally-arrogant, intellectually-smug Paul is no more – gone, finished, dead!! But I discovered and experienced the resurrection life of Jesus pulsating and vibrant within me – His strength for my weakness; His wisdom for my folly; His drive for my drift; His grace for my greed; His love for my lust; His peace for my problems; His joy for my sorrow; and His plenty for my poverty. Oh wonder upon wonder, Jesus not only reconciles me to God by His death but saves me, moment by moment, with His risen life.

You see, you not only start the Christian life by faith but it is by faith that you must go on. I'm not going back to the old way, Peter, by observing the rituals and the rules, and the regulations. Now Christ is living His God-life in me by His Holy Spirit, and I am letting Him do just that! God offered me life and I will not throw His gift back in His face by going back to fulfilling the impossible demands of the Law in my own strength. I resolutely and absolutely refuse to make the death of Christ on the Cross absurd, irrelevant and meaningless.

∼ CHAPTER 3 ∼

My dear brothers and sisters in Galatia, I want you to know how deeply I am concerned for you and bewildered in my mind as I think of you. It is not your sinfulness that troubles me but your stupidity. You have changed from trusting to trying; from believing to achieving; from receiving good news to responding to good advice; from your glorious delight in God to your grinding duty towards God; from accepting what God has done for you to attempting to earn God's favour by what you do for Him. I am completely mystified! The Peter-bug has infected you. I can only believe that something (or someone!) quite sinister has beguiled and mesmerised you.

When I came to you I spoke plainly and simply about God-come-to-earth, Jesus, who died on a Cross not as an example but as a Redeemer, and Saviour, and Freedom-giver. The Good News does not speak of a big 'do' but of a big 'done'. There's nothing more that we can do for Jesus did it all and we are complete in Him. It's not by works of righteousness but by His grace alone that we are complete in Him.

You know perfectly well that Calvary, where Jesus died, brought you to the end of yourself and sounded the death-knell of your ego forever. You became Christians with your ears not with your hands. In the light of all of this I need you to help me understand what is going on among you by answering this question – did you receive the Holy Spirit by trying to keep the Commandments or by believing what you were told?

I cannot understand why you would abandon something which was succeeding for something which has failed. It beggars belief that you would begin by letting God do what we desperately need Him to do and end up by doing it yourself – that you would substitute supernatural power for natural power having begun in the Spirit you now seem to be determined to continue in your own flesh. Forgive me for being so blunt with you – you must be absolutely crazy!!

When I think of all you went through – the accusations; the criticism; the opposition; the ostracism; the condemnation; the misunderstanding. What was all that about? Was it all unproductive and fruitless? Please, please, reflect on what happened among you. The powerful Spirit of the living God came upon you and worked among you and through you so that things were happening that human ability couldn't perform and the human mind couldn't explain. Human lives were transformed morally, spiritually, emotionally, psychologically, and physically. All of that happened not because you were trying to be good but because you listened to what was being said and you really believed what you heard. You know (oh, you know so well!) that that is the secret of it all – God fulfils what He promises and invariably means what He says.

This is not new teaching or flaky, fly-by-night theology. This is firmly rooted in Scripture. Let's go right back to the very beginning – to Abraham. How did he become a good man? He heard what God said and he responded with, 'God, I believe You!' I really want you to get a firm grip of this that the true sons of Abraham are neither Jews nor Arabs; neither circumcised nor uncircumcised; but those who say from their heart and with their will, 'God, I believe You!'.

Long ago God spoke in advance and made His intention clear that He would bring non-Jews into a living and right relationship with Himself not because of how they behaved but because of how they believed, and this is what Abraham is all about and where he fits into the picture. This was the incredible Good News that God shared with this seventy-five-year-old man all these years ago that the trust and obedience he demonstrated is the key to reality in our relationship with God.

Having blessed Abraham because of his submissive response, God assured him that the nations and the generations yet to be born would be blessed through him. This is unmistakably and plainly God's Plan, and the Bible records it with thrilling accuracy, that Abraham was called out to be the beginning of a spiritual nation and through this nation (the Jews) God would send His blessing to everybody. Can you really grasp this that the key to it all is not race but grace? The sheer undeserved favour and generosity of God.

Four hundred and thirty years later Moses appears on the scene and he is given the Law. However, the Law can never save a person because it can't cope with failure and it can never offer forgiveness. It demands absolute perfection without any lee-way or margin for error of any kind. The Law can't make anyone good – it can only show us and make us so aware of how bad we are. It rigorously and uncompromisingly tells us what to do and then punishes us when we fail to do what it demands.

Long ago, through a prophet called Habakkuk, God spoke with penetrating clarity. The Israelites had despised God and disregarded His Law and God revealed to Habakkuk that they would suffer punishment through the oppression and cruelty of the Babylonians. How on earth can they escape what they undoubtedly deserve? – By trusting God and living in obedience to Him and not just in their thinking about Him. You see, the Law is based on trying not on trusting. It's all there in the Old Testament – if we are trying to keep the rules we will have to live completely by the rules – and, frankly, that just doesn't work. But, wonder upon wonder, there is another way that totally delivers us from being religious and brings us into a living, vibrant relationship with God.

Jesus comes on the scene – out of eternity into history. He took into account both the promise given to Abraham and the Law given to Moses, because both came from God. In order to pass on the promise given to Abraham He took up the Law of Moses – He was born under the Law; was a son of the Law; was circumcised on the eighth day of His earthly life according to the Law; was taken to the Temple when He was twelve-years-of-age as prescribed by the Law; and until the day He died upon the Cross He kept in absolute perfection every last detail of the Law God had given.

The curse of the Law was upon Him not because He failed to keep it but because He did keep it in perfection and willingly and consciously accepted the punishment for everyone else's failure to keep it, so that they could go free. This is the amazing uniqueness of the Christian Good News – the Atonement (Jesus died in my place that I might have a living, vibrant relationship with God in time and through eternity!). This is the overwhelming glory of the Cross of Calvary – we are now free to live in the reality of God's promise to Abraham – whoever we are. That's why

Jesus cried out with His last triumphant, incarnational breath, "I've done it!!" So we now have the possibility and potential of a totally new way of living – whoever we are!! Now we can live the Jesus-life in the power of the Holy Spirit.

I realise that all of this sounds unbelievable and far-fetched and must seem to border on the realms of fantasy. So let me give you an illustration that might help you understand how wonderfully true all this is. Once a Will is made up in a proper way, and before authentic witnesses it is sealed and established – it now cannot be altered. The fact is that God unalterably sealed His Will to Abraham and to his offspring. I want you to notice that 'offspring' is singular and not plural. Only one male descendant of Abraham would share with him the promise God made to him. That one male offspring is unmistakably and incontestably Jesus Christ.

In the light of this, the Law – given more than four centuries later – can never negate the promise God made four hundred and thirty years earlier. The implication of this for you (and for all of us!) is that the overwhelming, profound, and eternal blessing of God, which is your spiritual inheritance, is not entered into by keeping the Commandments. If that were so then God's promise to Abraham and his 'Offspring' is absolutely worthless. Thrillingly God stands unalterably by His Last Will and Testament. So it is no longer down to us to try harder and do more but up to Him to fulfil what He so graciously promised. Our hope is no longer based on our performance but upon His promise.

You might well be asking where Moses and the Law fit in to all of this. You might well be feeling that I have so fused together Abraham and Jesus that I have shut out Moses and the Law. The fact is that some want to go to Christ without first meeting Moses and consequently they have no sense of sin. Without a sense of sin there can never be a sense of freedom. The reality is that everyone on this planet is held in terrifying custody by sin. The Bible affirms this with deeply disturbing and penetrating clarity. As we have already noticed, the Law has no power whatsoever to deliver us from sin's power and release us into the limitless floodtide of God's life. The function of the Law is not to bestow salvation – for that it cannot do – but to convince mankind of his need of it. God wants to take us to the Law; then through the Law into a glorious experience of the Promise. Jesus did not come either to destroy the Law or to supersede it – but to fulfil it, and so offer us God's spiritual inheritance by trusting in Him.

Before this momentous Good News broke upon our world – that we can find unbounded hope, vibrant life and unbelievable warmth and reality in a relationship with a holy God – the Law hopelessly enslaved us with its unachievable rules and regulations. Because of the despair and desperation which this caused we became alert and alive to the ongoing plan of God in His Son Jesus to redeem a people for Himself, and that this happens not by what we achieve but by how we believe; not by trying to be good but by trusting a good, overwhelmingly generous, lavish, and gracious God. What a Message!! We find peace with God not by the work we do with our hands but by the Word that He speaks into our ears. So the Law has done its job – making us aware of our condition and of God's concern.

Be absolutely assured that the only way into the family of God is by trusting in; depending on; and being committed to the perfect, unique, completed work of the God-incarnate Jesus, who died that we might live. The old self-life has forever gone because when He died we died with Him and so the old self-life is dead and buried. But death and the grave could not hold Him for God raised Him in resurrection power and we, too, share in that life-transforming, history-shaking reality – and baptism graphically and plainly portrays and proclaims that thrilling truth. Please realise that so far as salvation is concerned there are no barriers of race, social standing, or gender, for acknowledging the unconditional lordship of Jesus Christ is to become an heir of the Father and a joint-heir with His Son Jesus.

~ CHAPTER 4 ~

I know this is difficult for you to grasp but I really want you to understand that the Law of God is not an irrelevance that we can dismiss, or a fact the we can ignore and side-step. You see the Law does two things – it not only reveals sin, it also restrains sin. It cannot stop wrong-doing but it can put a brake on it to some extent. God did not give us the Ten Commandments to make us good; He gave them to us to show us how bad we are, and to stop us from getting worse.

In our Roman culture when you were young and immature you needed someone to be with you; to follow you around; to make sure you did not get into trouble. You needed a child-minder. The Law is God's moral and spiritual child-minder. The child may be the owner of a vast property but as a minor he can take no legal action nor make any legal decision. In reality he is not in control of his own life because everything is done and directed for him and he does what he is told.

But the time comes when his custodian or guardian passes him on to his father. At that time (between the age of 14 – 17years) the delegated authority to exercise discipline; to execute punishment; and to guard from danger is over and the father/son relationship becomes a reality. Mischievously, and with his own malevolent cunning, the devil took this good thing given for our benefit – the Law – and twisted it to his own evil purposes, in order to bring us into awful bondage.

God meant the Law to reveal sin and then drive us to His Saviour but the devil used the Law to reveal sin and drive us to despair. God meant the Law as an interim measure towards our justification but Satan uses the Law as a final step towards his condemnation. God meant the Law as a stepping-stone to freedom but Satan uses the Law as a blind-alley; a spiritual cul-de-sac where we get trapped and there is no way of escape.

However, God's hour has struck to set us free from our guardian and enter into His promised covenant-relationship with our heavenly Father.

91

Heaven has invaded earth; eternity has broken into history; the divine has become human in Jesus. Jesus, God's Son, is not only God's ideal man, He is also man's ideal God – His righteousness redeeming us in our unrighteousness.

In Him God dealt with our sin in order that we might become sons giving us a new Father and a new family. The Son of God became the Son of Man in order that the sons of men might become sons of God. Dear Galatian Christians, God sent forth His Son to give us the status of sonship, but He also sent forth His Spirit to give us the experience of sonship. What a God we have to want us not only to be aware of our salvation but also to be gloriously and truly aware of our sonship so that we now can speak to Him in the affectionate, confidential, warm, intimate language of a true son and not a terrified slave.

I find it so hard to understand how you can turn your back on all of this and go back to where you used to be. Knowing what you now know it is incomprehensible to me that you would return to rules and regulations that have no power whatsoever and consistently make you heavy-hearted because your freedom in Christ is not only curtailed but devastatingly crushed. You have exchanged life for legalism again. I certainly get the clear impression that you did not listen to a single word I said when I was with you.

I am begging you – even if you cannot listen to a word that I taught you – please, please, look at the life I am now living in glorious forgiveness and unbelievable freedom. You got to know me so well because you received me when I was flat on my back with a fever – but you couldn't have given me a warmer welcome had I come from heaven itself as a messenger of God. Although you did not know how to handle my sickness you never despised nor criticised me. In fact you could not have been more hospitable had I been the Lord Jesus Himself.

These were heady, happy days even though I was really struggling health-wise. You certainly made me aware that no sacrifice would have been too great for you to make for me – your care was unbelievable; your kindness unlimited; your generosity unbounded. The fragrance of that time permeates every memory I have of you. But everything seems to have changed – compassion seems to have been replaced with criticism; happiness replaced with heaviness; delight replaced with dullness; and straightforwardness replaced with suspicion. As far as I am aware the only thing I have done is to tell you the truth. I do realise that confronting error with truth can be intrusively painful, but I have done so not to hurt or harm you but to release you into glorious, spiritual freedom.

Those who have influenced and affected you have made much of you, so that you would make much of them – but the consequence of that is negative rather than positive and destructive rather than creative. Enthusiasm is good but it needs to have a right focus without being blurred and beguiled by wrong motives. It has always been my passion to make sure you were grounded on the firm and unshakable foundation of truth so that you would be able to stand firm and secure with your head held high whether I am present or absent.

You probably will never know how intensely I ache for you to make sure that you are truly born again and experiencing wonderful freedom and fullness in God through His Son, Jesus. At this moment I so want to be face to face with you so that you could see my body-language; be aware of the tenderness and tears in my eyes; and hear the longing and love in my voice. If only you knew how I feel about you. I confess I am at my wits end to know what to do.

I am certainly not sure that you recognise exactly what it really means for you when you not only say but also demonstrate that you prefer a religion of rules and regulations. You are sensible people who know the Scriptures – especially the Book of Beginnings. You will remember clearly that the accurate, indisputable, historical record says that Abraham had two sons born of different mothers. Hagar's son, Ishmael, was born as the natural process of conception, gestation, and, nine months later, birth. God had no part in it; never intended it; nor did He approve of it. Ishmael was the consequence of a human decision that led to a human action.

Sarah's son, Isaac, however, was born with a God-involvement that took him out of the realm of the normal process of human procreation and into the realm of divine promise. History affirms that one was purely natural and the other was powerfully supernatural. That is the reality of the situation that Scripture so clearly records.

That actual, historical record, however, can be understood in an allegorical way. These two sons with two mothers represent two religions one bringing mankind into bondage (Judaism) and the other bringing mankind into freedom (Christianity). You see, one of the loudest and proudest Jewish boasts is that Abraham was the founder and the father of their faith. But the important thing (in this situation) is not who your father is but who your mother is.

These two sons of Abraham, Ishmael and Isaac, took their character and destiny (in this situation) from their mothers rather than from their father. A slave girl can only have a slave boy. Ishmael was a slave boy because Hagar was a slave girl – even though his father was a free man. Hagar forever represents the Law and the capital city that demands we can only get right with God by keeping every rule and regulation in perfection with no exceptions whatsoever.

I realise that this is overwhelmingly offensive to every Jew – and I am a Jew myself – that to insist on getting right with God simply by keeping the Law means that you are descended from Ishmael. Our Lord Jesus Christ Himself taught so clearly that true descent from Abraham is not physical but spiritual; nor is it racial but regenerational. True descent from Abraham comes when you believe, as Abraham believed, and when you obey without reservation or restriction as Abraham obeyed.

When you insist on getting right with God by keeping the Law, you may well be descended from Isaac physically but you undoubtedly are descended from Ishmael spiritually. Sarah, however, stands for a new Jerusalem – a city not created and constructed by human ingenuity and endeavour; a city not of the present but of the future; not of earth but of heaven; not of bondage but of freedom. Seven hundred years before our Lord Jesus came into history the prophet Isaiah prophesied and proclaimed that very reality – which mother do you belong to and which city represents you?

Dear friends, can you not see this? You are in the family of God not because of your adherence to a demanding and impossible-to-keep programme but because of a declared and thrilling-to-receive promise. You are Isaac people! You know from the Scriptures that Ishmael scorned, mocked, and laughed at Isaac, and in the end he bullied him. There is no doubt that we, too, will experience hostility and pain and misrepresentation not only from the world but from our half-brothers – religious people – who belong to the I-must-be-good-in-order-to-get-to-heaven church.

Everyone who wants to earn God's favour by what they do will always be jealous of those who receive God's grace and undeserved favour because of who He is and what He has done in His Son, Jesus. There will always be tension between the natural and the supernatural. Natural religion with its habits; its customs; its observances; its adherence to rules and regulations; its activism; its good deeds will always be in conflict with supernatural religion which ministers joy because of a living, vibrant relationship made possible by the sheer, undeserved and unearned generosity of God's heart.

The Scriptures – in the Book of Beginnings – frighteningly say that there is an appointed day when Ishmael will be cast out. However, those who are truly born of the Spirit will inherit the Father's property and prosperity. The real division is not between Jew and Gentile but between living by faith and living by works; grace and Law; Spirit and flesh. In the light of all of this, get a grip, dearest friends, and claim your Isaac identity through recognising and receiving and responding to God's chosen One, Jesus, who became as we are so that we could become as He is – the Inheritor of God's promise – so setting us free forever from the law of sin and death.

~ CHAPTER 5 ~

Freedom is a basic human impulse and it certainly is one of the main keynotes in the ongoing march of history. It is one of the hardest things to get, yet it is one of the easiest things to lose – and you are in danger of losing it having so wonderfully found it. This is why I am writing this letter to you, with such overwhelming anxiety and with such unrestrained passion.

Freedom in itself is meaningless – and indeed can be destructive and dangerous – for it always has to be freedom for something. Jesus, the eternity-come-into-history One, has set us free not to do what we like or to surrender and conform to the restraints of others, but to become what God, our Father, always intended us to be – those who have entered into and experienced to the full what it means to be a child of God. So hear my cry: 'Do not budge one inch and allow yourselves to be hoodwinked and beguiled to return to the impossible task and crushing attempt to earn God's favour by trying to be good – for this is forever doomed to failure.

Listen with the utmost care and without distraction to what I am saying. The first thing I want you to notice is that false teachers emphasize the necessity of circumcision neither as a physical act nor a ceremonial rite but as a theological statement. Circumcision stands clearly as an evidence of a particular type of religion, which demands achieving rather than believing; works rather than grace; and trying rather than trusting.

If you accept this surgical procedure – over in a few minutes; healed in a few days – you will discover that it not only cuts off a part of your body from you, but cuts you off from Christ. The truth is that it is declaring that salvation requires more than faith in Jesus Christ and in Jesus Christ alone and consequently undermines His sole and absolute sufficiency. Please don't devalue and dismiss Christ in this way.

The second thing I want you to notice is the severe implication of the Law. If you want to get to heaven by keeping the Law you have to obey and live out every detail of the Law – you cannot pick and choose. It is not a question of getting so far by your own goodness and the rest of the way with God's grace. It is all or nothing – either all the way by your own effort or all of the way by God's grace.

You see some of you need to repent not only of your bad actions and thoughts and words but also of your good actions and thoughts and words as a means of securing salvation. By trying to reach a prescribed standard of goodness we put ourselves beyond the reach of God's grace – what an immense and devastating tragedy! So I want you to understand what a true Christian really is. He is a person whom God treats as good although he is bad because he has complete faith in the perfect, complete, and accepted-by-God work of Jesus Christ on the Cross of Calvary.

However, there is more to it than that. It is not just about the way that God treats me, it is also about the way God is involved in transforming me by His powerful, enabling Spirit to become more and more like His Son, Jesus. This is not some vacuous, insubstantial pipe-dream but a radiant certainty God has planted in our hearts. This is not something we work at but something we wait for daily with huge expectation. What is crucial is not just what we believe about Christ (although that obviously is important and fundamental!) but rather the reality of our faith in Christ even with the awesome frailty of our humanity. When that is established and real then neither circumcision nor uncircumcision is an issue.

Christianity is not just about a past encounter with Jesus but an ongoing, feet-on-the-ground, present-now-today walking with Him demonstrated in constantly wanting the best, the greatest, the most, the highest for those around me. Nor is Christianity a future expectation it is about a present unmistakable and unarguable evidence that you are now living the Jesus-life in the power of the Holy Spirit.

You were doing so well and I so admired what I saw. You were so concerned to behave as you believe. You were not satisfied with listening to God's Word you were determined to live God's Word. What happened? Who obstructed you and caused you to have a theology without experience. Anyone who influenced you in this way and beguiled you into thinking that you can't translate creed into conduct and Christian belief into Christian behaviour is not of God!

I need hardly remind you that a little off-centre-teaching has a massive effect not only on an individual, but on the fellowship of God's people there in Galatia. Nevertheless, in spite of what I have heard about you and the influences clearly at work among you I am thoroughly convinced that you will choose truth rather than error; a living relationship rather than a dead religion; and liberty rather than law. Be absolutely assured that there are dire consequences to anyone who deliberately distorts the truth, creating uncertainty where there should be certainty; causing frustration where there should be freedom; and challenging the revelation of God with the rules of men.

Dear Christian friends, it is ludicrous for anyone to suppose that you misheard and misunderstood what I taught you. I have consistently and straightforwardly taught you that Gentiles need not become Jews before they can be saved. I have with clarity and absolute conviction declared that our hope is built on nothing less than Jesus blood and righteousness. On Christ the solid rock we stand; all other ground is sinking sand. It is for this reason that Jesus surely did not die in vain and for this same reason I have suffered. I feel so strongly about this that I can only say that I wish that those who are attempting to create so much havoc among you would render themselves totally incapable of reproducing their kind.

To you, my dear friends, who stand absolutely complete in Christ, I must issue a clear and severe warning. You must not go from one extreme to the other. You must not go from your freedom from doing what others want you to do to imagining that you are now free to do what you want to do. Not only is the devil an extremist but our humanity, in its frailty, can beguile us into thinking that legalism has now been exchanged for licence and I am now free from all restraints so that I can follow my own inclinations; my own passions; my own feelings and emotions; and my own desires. God has not only given us the freedom not to sin, He has given us the freedom to care for others rather than ourselves and to be consistently compassionate towards them.

Please try to understand this for fear that you become like others and misrepresent me. You see there are two ways to end the Law – abolish it or fulfil it. To abolish it leads to chaotic anarchy; to fulfil it leads to compassionate, caring activity to bless and enrich the lives of others. It is to this that God calls us. If you ignore this then you will behave like animals for unbridled, uncontrolled human nature is totally destructive.

In the light of all of this, ask yourself the question: 'Who is in control of my life?' The answer to that question will decide what you do; how you react; and why you think the way you do. It is completely impossible for both the self and the Holy Spirit to be in control – they are mutually exclusive and as long as life on earth lasts constantly at war with one another. This is the reason for that constantly bewildering human situation that you know so well what you should say or do, but frustratingly seem unable to say it or do it.

The fact of the matter is that if every step you take; every decision you make; every thought you think; every emotion you feel; every motive you have is truly led by the Spirit of the living God, the Law no longer applies – and you are free at last!! You see, holiness is not an emotion, it is a decision and operates not in the area of your feelings but in the area of your will. The bold and blatant truth is that every one of us, as Christians, is as holy as he wants to be because the Good News of Jesus is not only that my sin can be totally forgiven but also I now have freedom to live a righteous life – His gift; my choice.

Let me spell this out for you – our lives, which could be a bridgehead for holiness can so easily become a bridgehead for hellishness. The dominion of darkness invades our lives sexually; religiously; emotionally; and socially. Sexually, promiscuity is never God's way. Indeed, chastity before marriage and fidelity within marriage was a completely new virtue Christianity brought into the world. Dirty-mindedness is like pus in an unclean wound and poisons and degrades everything wholesome that it touches.

Then there is a level of indecency which goes so low and so far in lust and perversion that the indecent person no longer cares what either God or man think or say but takes a reckless and audacious delight in shocking people. Such is the catalogue of sexual corruption when our unbridled human nature is given free rein. Religiously, human nature is prone to worship the things it has made – whether these are material or mental or moral images.

Also, man without God is exposed to deceptively disguised yet desperately destructive spiritual forces of darkness which ultimately lead to despair and dysfunctional living. Emotionally, the list is frightening – hostility; contentiousness; constantly discontented with what he has and constantly desiring what someone else has; prone to irresponsible and irrational outbursts of destructive anger; overwhelmed with self-seeking rather than serving others – grasping to get rather than generous to give; constantly critical and complaining causing fragmentation and conflict; creating little coteries of dissent and disapproval; and perhaps the meanest condition of all – an embittered mind – so much more sinister than straightforward jealousy.

Socially, mankind is constantly open to losing its discipline and self-control and living only to satisfy its baser instincts regardless of the impact on others around it, causing them embarrassment and discomfort. I cannot stress strongly enough, as I have already said, that to live this way comes at enormous cost – neglecting Kingdom-living now in history is to forfeit Kingdom-living in eternity. It stands to reason that if you cannot control your life properly in this world then there will be no invitation to share God's reign in the next.

However, there is another way made possible by the Spirit of the living God for, wonder upon wonder, He wants to form the very character of Jesus in us. The evidence of this is unconquerable benevolence; invincible goodwill – an attitude of mind and a determination of will which constantly seeks the highest good of every person. Dark despair is banished and a radiant vibrancy comes in its place.

A new sense of well-being is born, not because of self-effort, but as a result of God's undeserved favour and provision. A resilience emerges which refuses to give up too easily or give in too quickly and is determined to see things through. A sweetness of temper begins to show which puts others at their ease and shrinks from causing any unnecessary pain. Lavish, unstinted generosity is displayed in such a way and to such a degree that clearly God is the source. Instability goes and in its place a steady reliability takes over. God's authority is recognised and every instinct, passion, and impulse is brought under His control.

And finally you have a person who is able to say 'no' to himself and live with restraint and discipline. Note carefully that you cannot legislate for all of this – either you allow God to be God in you or it will never happen. Let's face it, the God-owned, Christ-controlled Christian will not tolerate in any shape or form the demands of the old way of living with its urgent, driving baser instincts. If we are now living the Jesus-life in the power of the Holy Spirit there must be incontrovertible and unmistakable evidence of this. Gone are the days when we cherished a vain illusion of ourselves challenging others to a dispute so that we can have an opportunity to prove that we are right or on the other hand being jealous of the attainments and gifts of others.

∼ CHAPTER 6 ∼

My dear friends, related to me so personally and deeply because of what Jesus Christ has so perfectly done for us on the Cross of Calvary, if surprisingly and embarrassingly you stumble on someone behaving or speaking in an inappropriate, ungodly and shameful way, because of your maturity in Christ, correct him and with sensitivity, patience and tenderness bring him to the place of repentance, where he can be put right with God and with others once more. But remember your own humanity and proneness to get things so wrong for fear that the very thing you correct in others is so blatantly obvious to others in you. The very judgment we pass on others can so easily become the judgment we tacitly pass on ourselves.

Be quick to see where others are struggling and get alongside them to share their load; identify with their anxiety; and empathize with their circumstances; for in this way you will display not only your love for another human being but also your love for God. Be careful not to become high and mighty in your own estimation of yourself as you occupy the moral high ground in your relationships with others when, in fact, you have no right to be there.

As human beings there is a constant tendency to be blind to the reality of our own situation. It is mandatory that we should be quick to shoulder our own responsibilities and take stock of our own motives, desires, and glaring imperfections before we mentor others into godliness. Then, and only then, can we begin to appreciate how much God has done and is doing so that we can feel comfortable in our own skin. It is unhelpful to feel good about ourselves as the result of the process of putting our lives alongside the life of another. We have more than enough on our own plate to sort out. However, as a result of recognising all of that in ourselves we are now in a position, with integrity and humility, to care enough for someone else by helping them into Christ-like living again.

Thank God for those who unpack God's Word in such a way as to make it understandable to you so that you can respond to it by living it in a life-transforming way. You have a responsibility to enrich those who have done this for you with the practical resources and provision that you can supply.

Be careful that you are not hoodwinked into believing you can pull the wool over God's eyes. God sees, hears, and is aware of every last detail that is going on in our lives. Be absolutely aware and completely assured that there is a powerful spiritual axiom which is constantly at work, not only in our world but also in our lives – it is the terrifying and inexorable law of sowing and reaping. Be sure that consistently and without fail you will reap what you sow.

Any one of us who feeds our natural tendency to live in an ungodly, selfish, earth-bound way with little regard for God's laws, God's desires, and God's intentions for us is in deep trouble and is well on the way to pushing the self-destruct button. On the other hand any one of us who feeds the new life that has been gloriously born within us, by the powerful and precious Holy Spirit of the living God, has an indescribable hope and an unimaginable future.

In the light of all of this continue to be eager and enthusiastic in your concern and commitment to bless and enrich others in a positive and creative way, for that law of sowing and reaping never stops whatever our circumstances. There will always be rich consequences rewarding our persistence and perseverance to bless others no matter how we feel. So keep up the good work and make those who are in God's family your priority when it comes to blessing others.

This is no formal letter dictated to focus on such an important theological issue as our freedom in Christ. Its contents are vital but I want you to receive it in a deeply personal way and that is why I have not dictated it but written it myself, although my eye-sight these days leaves a lot to be desired.

At the risk of repeating myself and boring you I wanted to return to the nub of the matter in hand once again. There are those among you who are determined to return to legalistic religion rather than revel in a living relationship with God through His Son, Jesus. It is offensive to them to acknowledge that we will never get right with God by doing what we do rather than depending on what He has so perfectly and undeservingly done. This is not only personally humbling but is culturally offensive. It is for this reason that the Cross of Calvary sticks in their throats.

The fact of the matter is that it is not humanly possible, with absolute honesty and integrity, to fulfil every last legal requirement of Judaism. The reason that so much pressure is being brought to bear on you is not for your benefit but rather that their prejudice, pre-conceived ideas, and personal pride can be satisfied as you turn back from living truth and follow paralysing tradition once more. I so much want you to know that forever at the very centre of all that I am, and all that I do, and all that I have is the Cross of Calvary where God become flesh; eternity descended into history; the divine, made human, died and I died with Him so that every blandishment; every pressure; every influence; every incentive; every desire for reputation; every reward that the world has to offer is now gone forever.

I no longer have any concern for any religious practice of any kind. All that matters to me now is that new, liberating life has been born within me enabling me to live the Jesus life in the power of the Holy Spirit. Literally, that is precisely what I am about. May limitless well-being and the unhindered, unearned favour of God rest not only on those who have truly grasped this magnificent message of freedom, but have also seen it modelled in flesh and blood reality in my life. Because I am a Jew myself my heart aches particularly for those who are struggling with some other way to find peace with God.

Because of my very real humanity I wanted to share a final request with you. I would be so grateful that as a result of what I have written to you I would not reap a further whirlwind of invasive persecution, for my body is already weakened, sore, and broken through deprivation and corporal punishment, involving savage beatings as a consequence of taking a firm and open stand for what Jesus has so perfectly done and for what He has so plainly taught.

May the sheer, undeserved favour and generosity of our Lord Jesus Christ be real and active, not just in your minds but in the deep places of your being affecting profoundly not just how you think but how you live, day by day, my dear, precious family.

May it really be so!!

THE GOD-LIFE AND ITS CONSEQUENCES

Paul's Letter to the

Ephesians

Paul's Letter to the

EPHESIANS

~

THIS IS A LETTER FROM PAUL – yes, that's right, the same man who was at Ephesus for a while and who used to be called Saul of Tarsus, the religious, self-righteous fanatic who ruthlessly and violently opposed the Church. Incredibly, I have been sent out to share the message of Jesus Christ because that is what God had in mind for me to do. This letter is written to those who believe in Jesus; behave like Jesus; and belong to Jesus not only in Ephesus but in the surrounding countryside.

May you all know the sheer underserved generosity and unrestricted well-being of the God who really exists, who is also our Heavenly Father and Jesus Christ who came into history out of eternity to be the Lord of our lives.

Give unreserved thanks to this God who not only really exists, but who always is and always has been in a close, intimate, and personal relationship with His Son Jesus Christ our Lord. He has enriched our lives beyond our wildest imagination in the unseen, yet unmistakably real, world, which is not restricted by time and space, with every conceivable treasure because of the faithfulness of His Son Jesus and our utter dependence on Him.

This God of ours had plans for us even before the land and sea, sky or nature came into existence. This plan is that because of His Son we should be pure and without fault in His righteous eyes. Because of His amazing love – which defies human understanding – God decided of His own accord that though we had no relationship with Him we would have a deep, family relationship with Him because of His only real Son, Jesus. This was the result of the delight in His heart over us and His divine decision to do something about our estrangement from Him.

No wonder we are ecstatic with joy and gratitude because of His brilliant, undeserved generosity which has flowed towards us without restriction because of His dear Son Jesus whom He loves. Wonder of wonders, we have not only been set free from all that hinders and restricts our true humanity because Jesus died that we might live as God created us to live, but we have also been given a new beginning, a clean sheet of paper, so that there is nothing any longer that makes us guilty because of the sheer, underserved generosity of God's heart.

This incredible thing that grips us is that we can now begin to see things from God's point of view and grasp God's real agenda for us. He has taken us aside and shown us what He alone knew about His eternal intentions because He is that kind of God. He has done all of this because at the right time Jesus came and made it possible to unite in history what God had always intended in eternity.

Because of Jesus we are now here on earth at this time not by chance but by choice (His choice), whatever the circumstances of our birth, heredity or environment so that God might fulfil His agenda perfectly in us. He has done this so that all in heaven and on earth might lavishly and profoundly express their thankfulness for His comprehensive completeness and indescribable brilliance.

So, those of you who are reading this letter must realise that you, too, became part of this God-plan the moment you heard, grasped, and believed what God had done for you in His Son Jesus. He brought you into a living, vibrant relationship with Himself; setting your feet on a road that would bring pleasure to Him, and giving you a hope that not even death can destroy.

God did something excitingly wonderful in that moment of honesty as you stubbornly faced the actual reality of your situation apart from God – He identified that you, indeed, were His and His life burst forth in you (transforming, life-changing life that delivered you from religion and gave you reality). Something began in you in history that one day will be perfected in eternity – so that men and angels will worship this God for His comprehensive completeness and indescribable, shadowless light.

Because of this incredible Good News about God and from God which I have just shared with you, I cannot tell you how overwhelmingly grateful I am that you have found this reality to be true in your own lives as you have encountered the risen Lord Jesus Christ and responded to Him, not just in your heads but in the obedience and commitment of your lives day by day. The other thing that delights me is what I have heard about your attitude towards other followers of Jesus – wanting always and only the best, the most, and the highest for them.

As I pray for you my heart is warmed and I constantly ask that God, revealed in our Lord Jesus Christ not only to be transcendent above and beyond us but immanently close and intimate with us, will enable you to see things from His point of view and to receive from Him with certainty what He shows you supernaturally by His Spirit, so that you will get closer and closer to Him. I am praying, too, that deep down in the core of your being, beyond how you think and what you feel, you will grip the certainty of what lies ahead for you immediately and in the future. I am talking about the eternal birthright of all who know the re-creating

110

and resourcing power of the Holy Spirit who is strong with a strength impossible to calculate.

We catch a glimpse of this power as we watch God at work taking the broken, shattered body of His Son Jesus triumphantly from the grave and enabling Him to take His place in the throne-room of the universe, incalculably superior to anything or anyone in history and in eternity. From that kingly throne He reigns and demonstrates His lordship over everything, so that His new Body on earth can, without hindrance, declare and demonstrate who He is and what He does without any limitation at any time and in every place.

∼ CHAPTER 2 ∼

You know this is true – your physical bodies were alive; your minds, your emotions, and your will were alive; but the spiritual part of you was dead, overwhelmed by conscious and unconscious self-interest, self-indulgence, and self-gratification. You were victims and prisoners to both seen and unseen forces which beguiled and manipulated you so that you ignored and discarded the purposes of God.

I know that this is true since all of us, as human beings, have lived this way – helpless and vulnerable to godlessness. The beauty of the natural world around us and the reality of the moral law within us drew us to God but we turned our backs blatantly on Him. The result is that His righteousness, justice, and holiness were offended and His retribution overflowed upon us. We had not learned that rebellion leads to retribution and repentance leads to restoration. Yet, thank God, He did not give up on us even though we continually justified our attitudes and behaviour.

His persistent love relentlessly pursued us, because that is the kind of God He is – our hope lies in His character not in our conduct. He saw us as we are and did something about it. He sent the Lord Jesus Christ into the world so that by His death we might live. The dead part of us

(I wrote about that earlier in this letter) could now live – not because of what we could do but because of the sheer, undeserved generosity of His heart in doing what He did. From being nothing, He made us something in Jesus – not only to live with Christ's life but to reign with Him in the place of victory and authority so that future eternal generations could see His limitless, beyond compare, unearned generosity in wretched, hopeless, helpless people like us.

We have been brought into vibrant new life because of God's sheer, undeserved generosity – and it has become ours by our exercise of faith in what Christ has done for us. God has given us this new life; all we have to do is receive it!

It doesn't make us better than anyone else for it has nothing to do with us and everything to do with Him. I cannot get over this – God Himself has made us as we are physically, psychologically, intellectually, socially, and emotionally so that we are uniquely special to Him and He has a specific role for us to fulfil in this life that no one else could ever fulfil. It is a role that is relevant, effective and fruitful and it has always been in God's mind for us only. Because of this there is no need – ever, for you or me, to imitate someone else.

All of this is even more wonderful since, racially, you were not Jews by birth and were despised as 'Law-breakers' (the evidence of which they carry in their bodies because the 'open' marks of Judaism were observing the Sabbath and being circumcised!). So, at that time, neither did you know God's grace nor, by race, did you have any part with God's people since you had no part in the promise God had made to the father of the faithful, Abraham, securing His relationship with His own people the Jews.

To put it bluntly neither God nor man could help you and despair and darkness loomed ahead of you like a bottomless chasm. But this is the wonder of it all that you who were in a spiritual desert far, far away from God have been brought into a spiritual oasis of vibrant relationship with God through what Jesus the Messiah did for you on Calvary's Cross.

This same Jesus, out of conflict brings reconciliation; out of division brings oneness; out of separation brings at-one-ment. He did this by exchanging the law with its impossible demands of rules and regulations for a living relationship through His perfect, sinless life on earth and His redemptive, atoning death for us and for everyone everywhere. This is why He came – this God-man – not only to unite Jews and non-Jews but also to unite both with God; that the divine and the human, the flawed and the faultless, God and man could at last be in present, perfect relationship. At Bethlehem Jesus brought God to man but at Calvary He brought man to God. Jesus came for all of us whether we have a non-religious or a religious background. Now the door of heaven is open and no one can close it because Jesus has opened it.

What a result!! No longer separated by race or religion but Kingdom people now; family now, brothers and sisters with the same Father now. The ground of our security is that God has taken the initiative and in His powerful and authoritative Word has pointed backwards in the New Testament and forwards in the Old Testament to Jesus, the Messiah. Jesus is the One who is our refuge, our hiding place, our shelter, our protection and the source and focus of our worship.

Because of Him you, too, are being built into a community in which God lives and through which God reveals Himself – for God no longer lives in buildings but in people who have been gloriously set free from their old way of living by His Son and day by day are now living – both corporately and individually – in a way that cannot be explained in human terms by His Spirit.

∼ CHAPTER 3 ∼

Because of this, I pray for you all although I am now chained to a Praetorian guardsman – but my real captor is Jesus who met me, confronted me, challenged me, changed me and commissioned me on the Damascus Road to be His ambassador and spokesman to give you non-Jews a hope and a future.

You must have heard somewhere, somehow, that God took this violent opponent of His Son and transformed him through His sheer, undeserved generosity so that same generosity could be yours too. This is what this letter is all about – God showing me what He is really like and making me realise that I can have a living relationship with Him, not by being religious and slavishly adhering to and obeying a whole list of rules and regulations, but by trusting in and depending on what He has done in His Son Jesus. Hard as it is for conscious humanity to grasp this, it is the truth which God alone can declare – and He has taken the initiative and declared it to me. Hopefully this letter will help you grasp this revealed secret from God.

Generations past wondered, hoped, and then dismissed all this too good to be true. However, they wonder no longer because the Spirit of God has taken some of the people of God and shown them the liberating Good News of God. Of course, you have now grasped that this Good News in a bad news world is wonder upon wonder, and every wonder true. You are joined with God's own people, the Jews, without restriction or limitation, in Christ's new Body on earth – the Church – sharing all the blessings and benefits God promised so long ago through His faithful servant, Abraham, as you believe in Jesus, behave like Jesus, and belong to Jesus.

I am what I am because God is what He is, I have absolutely nothing to commend me because of the way I have behaved. God's people have every reason to despise me and God has every reason to distrust me and even destroy me but He didn't – Oh, how the grace of God amazes me.

He took me from my sin and set me free. What greater things could be given to a legalistic, prejudiced Jew than to share the limitless, lavish blessing of Jesus Christ and His Kingdom with non-Jews and to assure everybody, Jews and non-Jews alike, that this is what God has called and commissioned me to, although past generations were unable to experience and enjoy this incredible reality for which God is responsible.

Although the Jews will always have a special place in God's unfolding agenda, the Church is God's ultimate achievement. It is through this new Body of His Son on earth that He has decided, at this present time, to reveal with unmistakable clarity the many-faceted realities of His purposes and plans to the hierarchy of spiritual beings in the unseen world.

This has always been in His mind and on His agenda but it has come into being now because His Messiah has lived and died among us and now reigns over us. It is because of our new life in Jesus, made real for us by trusting in Him, because of who He is and because of what He has done, that we can freely and boldly come into the presence of a Holy God. You know that I am in prison today for your sake, but do not let that put you off because my imprisonment is so that you might be free.

And now I want to go back to where I was before I got side-tracked by the astonishing wonder of God's grace – grace that triggers something within me that is like an irrepressible fountain that cannot be contained – that He would use a man like me to share such incredible things with you!! Because of this I pray for you – not some formal, cursory prayer that I used to pray as a Jewish religious man on my feet, with my hands extended towards God, palms up – but a longing, yearning, urgent prayer, on my knees, crying to God who is the Father of all who have been born again into His family, whether they are still living on earth or they have gone to be with Him; Jews or non-Jews.

My prayer is that out of the limitless depths of His goodness, His grace, and His blessings you would know what it means to be naturally supernatural and supernaturally natural because His Holy Spirit is at work unseen – but, oh, so obviously real – in and through you. My prayer is that His Holy Spirit would credit you with the risen life of His Son and that you would give our Lord Jesus unhindered access to every area of your life, both seen and unseen, trusting Him where you find it so difficult to let go your old ways of thinking and living.

Believe me, when I say that I pray that Calvary love (released in you by the Holy Spirit) would grip you so deeply and so strongly that you, along with all those who believe in Jesus, would have the ability and the security of knowing the extravagant, lavish, immeasurable, beyond-our-capacity-to grasp love of Jesus, the Messiah – and in doing so have your whole being, body, soul, and spirit, overflowing with God.

I want to ascribe honour and majesty to this God of ours who goes far beyond the most and the highest we can ever think, and beyond the widest borders of our imagination because the same power that raised Jesus from the dead is at work in us. Bow before Him; lift your hands to Him; surrender your lives to Him so that His fullness and His radiance might be staggeringly seen among and through His people and in His Son now at this time and in generations that are yet to be – and so through eternity when time and space will be no more.

～CHAPTER 4～

So far this letter has been about two things. First, the astounding, amazing, extravagant grace of God for all who will respond to it whatever their background. Second, that this God would want someone like me, of all people, to be made aware of this and then to share it with others. Because of this I have landed up in prison.

However, that sheer, undeserved generosity of God needs to have shoes on its feet and clothes on its back so that it can be seen and understood in the real world. Truth believed needs to be truth behaved otherwise it is not really truth believed. Unless this truth radically and intrusively affects our life-style and the way we live, it is completely irrelevant and utterly useless. So, hear the longing and the yearning of my heart that you would take this seriously and be completely different people from what you used to be.

How are you to do this? By stopping all your attempts at trying to be good and letting God do what He wants to do both in you and through you. This is a revolutionary and comprehensive life-change and does not come easily to any of us because of our proud hearts. We need consciously and deliberately to move over from the driving seat of our lives and allow God to be responsible for the direction we now take. It is not that we lose any of the distinctiveness, vitality or creativity of our personality – not at all – but now it is under God's control.

Having understood that, we then need to have a new attitude to others – particularly when we find them irritating, awkward and intruding into our lives. This is a constant attitude that makes allowances for other people's faults – a tall order unless and until all that I have written already becomes vibrantly real in our lives. You see, it is not at all difficult to be a Christian! It is utterly impossible without the enabling and vitality of the Holy Spirit.

The Holy Spirit is not responsible for dividing Christians – it is sin that does that! He is responsible for uniting Christians at a depth and a reality we have never known before. Our responsibility is not to achieve or create unity – that's what the Holy Spirit does ! Our responsibility is to protect, guard and maintain the unity that the Holy Spirit gives. There is only one Body of Christ on earth; and only one Holy Spirit. He is the One who makes Jesus real to us and delivers us from darkness and despair, giving us a future that is unbelievably attractive and wonderful.

You see there is only one Lord –one God, come-in-the-flesh, Jesus. There is only one way to obtain God's pardon and His promises and that is by faith alone. There is only one way to declare and demonstrate that the old you is not only dead, but is buried; and the new Christ-resurrection-life living in you is triumphantly real, and that is by baptism.

From all I've been saying you now know there is only one God and He is Father to all who have realised their lives are far away from pleasing Him; have repented of this reality; and have responded to His call to come under His rule and authority in His Kingdom. Because He is our Father we now have many brothers and sisters in His family.

However, although we have been brought into a new, close, united relationship with one another, there is diversity too. The Lord Jesus has seen fit to give gifts to each one of us without exception. These gifts do not demonstrate the love He has for us, but clearly demonstrate the purpose He has for us. That's why it says in the Old Testament that when Jesus ascended from the Mount of Olives to be with His Father, in the throne room of the universe, He asked His Father not only to send His Spirit upon us, but also to equip and resource us divinely and supernaturally to function properly and effectively in His new Body, the Church.

When we speak about Jesus' ascension it makes us realise the glory and splendour He left in order to be with us on earth and also the depths to which He went when He invaded the territory of the departed spirits. Yes, this same Jesus who did this ascended beyond our ability to understand or grasp in order to fulfil His cosmic purpose and mission.

It was Jesus who decided that some should be church-planters – spiritual architects, who have His blue-print, giving details and directions to His people so that they will know what they should do, and how they should relate and develop together. He also decided who should have a listening-ministry – hearing what God thinks; knowing what is on God's agenda; feeling God's emotions; and speaking out simply and clearly regardless of personal cost.

Others are to be spiritual obstetricians making sure that spiritual babies are born properly. Still others have the responsibility of taking God's written, powerful, and authoritative Word and making it clear, understandable and practical so that God's people will know what God wants and how they are to live. Then there are those who Jesus wants to be spiritual paediatricians who will make sure that the spiritual babies that are born will be given the right environment, circumstances and food so that they will grow up strong and healthy and become mature. All these gifts are given by the risen Lord Jesus to cause His new Body on earth to function properly, declaring His Word simply and demonstrating His life clearly.

The ultimate aim of these gifts given to people, is to make His new Body strong and resilient with all its members living in harmony; developing in maturity; and being aware of who He really is so that the world might see and hear what He is really like too.

Childishness, pettiness, superficiality and selfishness have no place among God's people. Neither has gullibility so that they are constantly at the mercy of those who want to seduce, beguile and manipulate them for their own selfish purposes and pretentious arrogance. No, no, God's people are to grow up and become mature together.

This maturity will be seen in three distinctive principles. **First** of all, every individual within the family of God will be in an unhindered and right relationship with Jesus, the Head of the Body, His Church. **Secondly,** each one of God's people, without exception, will be in the place God has put them fulfilling the function for which He has gifted them. **Thirdly,** every individual will be in a right relationship with one another. The love that the Holy Spirit alone makes possible and actual, will flow in all of this cementing, securing, creating, releasing and enabling. This is what delights the heart of God.

Please, please hear the cry of my heart as I write to you, don't on any account live the way you used to, without God and without hope in the world. Your minds, at that time, were focused on things that have no substance and you were deluded. The light of God had not yet shone into the recesses of your personality and the life of God had not yet been born in you since you had set your faces stubbornly against Him. Darkness and hardness had beguiled you from being truly human and had caught you up in an insatiable cycle of gratifying your body with all kinds of perversion.

But all this has changed now that Jesus has met you and given you a completely new life-style – a life-style based on truth not error; on reality not on fantasy; on God not on man. You have come to realise that there must be a complete break with the past that almost destroyed you with its beguiling drivenness. It had to begin with a change of mind that led to a change of heart that led to a change of motive, attitude and life-style. You have now broken through to a totally new way of life that neither you, nor others, would ever have believed to be possible. You are now realising the purpose for which you were born – that God wants to reproduce His life in you and through you so that the rest of creation might begin to realise what He is really like.

So, please pay careful attention to the fact that salvation is not simply an event in the past, it is a life-style for every day that you live. Here are some of the things that will show that you really are redeemed. Telling lies of any kind must be completely outlawed in your life – whether it is in what you say or in what you don't say. It is so easy to tell the truth but not the whole truth. This is always true but it has particular relevance for you when you are dealing with others in the church.

There are times when it is right to be angry but learn to distinguish your motives in being angry for fear that your anger is inappropriate and unacceptable in the sight of God. I urge you not to allow your anger to smoulder on lest it burns you up inside and becomes something which the enemy of your soul can use to his own advantage.

Taking what does not belong to you must stop even though, somehow, you feel you can justify what you are doing because of your need. If you have a need that must be met, then find some way that is creative and helpful to others, so that you can earn enough not only to meet your need but also to have something left over to share with others.

Watch your language and always ask yourself if what you are about to say is both true and necessary to say at that particular moment and in that particular context before you say it. Encouragement is normally expressed in our words but our unguarded and insensitive words can bring so much discouragement. Learn to affirm and commend one another rather than undermine and criticise one another. Be constantly aware that the Holy Spirit is a Person not a thing or an inanimate force or power.

Powerful though He is, He is also tender and sensitive towards us and never takes advantage of anyone. So take care not to hurt Him by living as if He did not exist or by your stubborn hard-heartedness that silences His voice because you want your own way. He is the One who has put God's trade-mark on you for eternity – when justification and sanctification are completed in glorification.

Dismiss any sour or unforgiving attitude to any other person; outbursts of uncontrollable anger must go; hurting others by throwing your weight about must go; destroying someone's good name must go; any other kind of damaging vindictiveness in the way you live or in things you say must go.

Instead of all these negatives go out of your way to be gentle, thoughtful, sensitive, and practically caring to one another. God has forgiven you so much it is surely not unreasonable for you to do the same to others.

∼ CHAPTER 5 ∼

If I could sum all this up it would be to say to you: allow the God-life in you to be expressed through you!! Realise that your identity and your security are in Jesus who loves you, as you are, with an unconditional love. Nothing you could ever say or do could make you more loved by Him than you are right now at this very moment. Remember this is not a soft, sentimental, erotic love but it is a self-giving, no axe-to-grind, sacrificial love. This is what brought so much pleasure to the Father-heart of God and this is the way He wants you to love others – giving not getting; generous not grudging; and serving not selfish.

I am returning to specifics again so that you would be in no doubt about salvation being a new life-style and not just a past event. After all, dying for you was the most He could do, so living for Him is the least you can do.

Chastity outside of marriage and fidelity within marriage are no-argument-absolutes for you who belong to Jesus. Being content and satisfied with having your needs met is foundational to a Christian life-style. Anything less than this, however you might justify it to yourselves and others, is inappropriate and unacceptable for God's people. The standards, ambitions, and aspirations of the world are not yours.

Forgive me for returning yet again to the way we speak but this is so indicative of the kind of people we are. Vulgar, crude and insensitive words have no place in your vocabulary nor does blue humour of any kind. Instead, we should be quick to express gratitude for God's goodness and grace in a spontaneous, sincere and unaffected way.

Let's get this straight, once and for all, there needs to be visible evidence of a life-style that demonstrates that you are now under God's authority and rule. Inappropriate and unacceptable relationships, behaviour, and speech, as well as dissatisfaction with what you already have, expresses more loudly than words that you are serving another master who is neither God nor His Christ. We are not playing verbal games here but we are dealing with a holy and almighty God who will not tolerate words which have no content or a theology based on sentiment rather than on Scripture. Have nothing to do with any of that stuff!

There was a day when life was a mystery without destiny and you did and said whatever you liked. But now you have discovered the real reason why you were born, why you are here, and what lies ahead. Because of this live in a way that is proof of that discovery – doing what is right but always with tenderness and humility; living in a right relationship with God but always with compassion and concern for others; adhering to and honouring God's absolutes but always trying to understand why others find that to be difficult.

In all of this our main concern is to bring pleasure to the heart of God rather than being well-thought-of. So shun everything that hurts Him, and make sure that others know that He can be hurt. God has called you to live transparent lives whether in public or in private; seen or unseen; in secret or in full view of the whole world; for nothing can ever be hidden from God. This is why the Church is constantly singing:

> 'The night is past; the day has come;
> Where darkness reigned; the light has shone.
> Our Christ in resurrection life appears;
> His presence banishing primeval fears.'

So watch your step day by day – no longer as those who are ignorant but as those who know precisely where it is at. In every circumstance; in every context; in every situation; do what honours God because there are so many who wander, disorientated, in the dark. If you are going to live this way you must realise you will never do it on your own no matter how committed and enthusiastic you are.

You know that alcohol changes your behaviour, often making you unpleasant and objectionable. You have been there and done that, but these days are completely different. There is another Spirit who also changes our behaviour and you need to be constantly and completely intoxicated with Him. He will affect your relationships with others, encouraging rather than discouraging them; healing rather than hurting them; blessing rather than burdening them. He will also affect your relationship with God our Father and His Son, our Lord Jesus Christ. Your attitude to Them will be wonder, worship, and gratitude for even the smallest and seemingly most insignificant things you experience.

Because you want to honour our Lord Jesus your attitude will always be one of willing, voluntary, releasing submission in your relationships with others. Arrogance, aggressiveness, standing up for your rights will not be characteristic of your behaviour. This will affect your marriage; your family life; and the way you earn your living.

Wives, give up your rights and get a hold of your responsibilities to your husbands as if they were Jesus Christ, your Lord and Master. You see God has an order for marriage, not only for partnership and parenthood but also for a prophetic dimension to be declared. It is because of this that wives are asked to submit to their husbands since God intended that the husband should be the head of the wife in the same way that Christ is the Head of the Church.

Obviously, a headless body can never function. So God took the initiative and sent His Son to be the Head of His new Body on earth, the Church. A church that is relevant and effective can only be so as it recognises and responds to Jesus Christ as Lord. To declare and demonstrate this, God gave marriage this prophetic dimension so that creation – both seen and unseen – should know this. The wife is to represent the Church (the people of God) and the husband is to represent Christ. What a thrilling, cosmic dimension God intends for marriage!! Don't devalue, downgrade, or denigrate it.

Husbands, give up your rights and get a hold of your responsibilities to your wives. I have addressed wives first but I have much more to say to husbands. You are to love your wives with a selfless, serving, sacrificial love that Jesus displayed when He died on the Cross. This is how Jesus loved the Church; and this is your inescapable pattern, husbands. Jesus did what He did to enable the Church to become what He always intended she should be. He did this by washing her clean (symbolised in baptism) through His cleansing, redeeming love and resurrection life as affirmed in the powerful and authoritative Word of God.

Jesus always had in mind that one day He would be the Bridegroom and the Church would be His bride – unspoiled by the environment of a fallen world; unaffected by the long years of her history; and unstained by anything that would disqualify her from being the bride of Christ.

What an incredibly tall order for any husband who reads this and sincerely wants to honour God in his marriage. So, practically, to bring it down to earth, husbands need to be as conscious and as caring for their wives as they are for their own bodies. In a word, loving your wife is simply like loving yourself. Frankly, this is not too difficult to grasp because our own bodies are always there to be lived in and we do everything possible to make them comfortable, healthy, effective, satisfied, and safe. We use a lot of time, give a lot of consideration, spend a lot of money, take a lot of care in order to do that.

That is how Jesus relates to the Church – it is the focus of His attention and so He provides for, protects, and resources her. You must know this by now because you are members of the new Body of Christ on earth, His Church. You see, marriage is God's idea, and it is for this magnificent cosmic purpose that a man will make a complete break with his secure social environment and take responsibility for a completely new way of life. He will enter into a unique, inseparable relationship with a woman, sealed and secured sexually, so that two human beings become one human being.

How can you possibly explain such a relationship in a way that the human mind will be satisfied? Actually, you can't until you realise this God-dimension in marriage – it's about the staggering, intrusive, intimate relationship that God's Son wants to have with God's people. So back to the practicalities of living a life in the power and purposes of God in the context of marriage, husbands. You are to want the best, the most, the greatest, and the highest for your wife, using as a yardstick what you would want for yourself.

Now a final word to the wife. You are to recognise marriage as God intended it to be and so respond to, and release your husband to be the man God requires him to be.

～ CHAPTER 6 ～

Of course we know that parents exist for their children and not the other way round. However, children have responsibilities too in the agenda of God. Their responsibility is to respond positively in obedience to their parents whom God has given them to care for them, to correct and control them. They are to do this not because parents are always right but because this is what God wants them to do.

Long, long ago God spoke about the importance of our attitudes to and our relationship with Him. He went on to speak about our attitudes to and our relationship with those around us. God not only communicated with His people but actually gave orders and commanded them so that they would be left in no doubt about what He wanted and how they should live.

You see, what He said was not an option but was an obligation. Having spoken about our relationship with Him, He then spoke about the first context in which we relate to those around us – the home. It is so logical – how can we live the God-life in society if we cannot live it at home? Our attitude to those around us begins by respecting and responding to those who gave us life and who are concerned about the way we live it.

There's a special word I have for fathers here – because they carry the ultimate responsibility for the climate, character, and condition of the family. Just as children have responsibilities so do fathers. His task is to make sure that his children grow up in an environment which is positive not negative; creative not destructive; encouraging not frustrating. He is also responsible for defining and then displaying God-values.

Having spoken of marriage and family life, let's go on moving outwards. The world of work is a crucial context for living the God-life. So here are some instructions and guide-lines. Employees, you are to respond to those for whom you work as you would respond to Christ. Honour them and be concerned to please them and fulfil their expectations of you. Work this way, without doing one thing and saying something entirely different to those around you. Be consistent!

Don't ever be 'eye-servants' but remember God sees what others never see and He knows what others will never know – your motives, your intentions, and your desires. I cannot stress too strongly how important it is that you work for others in such a way that God would be pleased with your efforts. When all is said and done you are no longer doing anything to increase your bank balance, but to please God who is the best Master and gives the best pay-cheque.

And now a word to employers, for socially and traditionally you are expected to stand up for your rights but you have responsibilities like everyone else under the Lordship of Christ. What I have just written to employees in the Name of Jesus I want you to have the same God-attitude. Never be overbearing or bullying, throwing your weight about because of your position. Remember that you, like them, are sinners saved by the grace of God and you are accountable to Christ before whose Judgement Seat one day you will stand. Jesus is the One who will pass judgement on all of us, you included, for the way we have lived here on earth. Remember He sees us not as employees or employers but as people.

That's about it, really. All that remains for me to say is remember what it means to be a Christian. It is not about you; it is about Christ. It's not about you trying harder but rather about you trusting more – allowing God to be God in you and through you. What I have just been saying to you will never be possible if you try to live this way in your own strength. Only God can do this – and He wants to and He will if you let Him.

Almost my final word to you is that you have entered a spiritual dimension which is not only exhilarating and exciting but is also dangerous. You must realise that you will never again be civilians – there's a war on and people get wounded and even killed on the battlefield. So, take advantage of all the equipment God gives you so that you can remain on the front line rather than in the field-hospital or even worse get mortally wounded.

Please, please realise what you are really up against – it is not flesh-and-blood humanity but rather the organised, powerful, and demonic hierarchy of evil which may well be invisible to us but is vicious, destructive, and corrupting nevertheless. So you are going to need everything you can get from God to protect and arm you when the storm breaks upon you from the dominion of darkness.

Do not be afraid when this happens; God's presence and provision is more than adequate to keep you on your feet – defiant and strong. Don't run from the enemy; resist him. In order to do this you will have to stand firm in the truth God has shown you so that you will never be a victim of Satan's lies. You will need to make sure that there is no unconfessed sin in your heart so that you are pure and holy because of what Jesus has accomplished for you on the Cross.

A dominating priority will need to possess you – to go out and declare and demonstrate the Good News so that God's peace will shine through you and from you, and be a light in the disorder and darkness to all you encounter. You will also need an unshakable confidence in our God who is absolutely trustworthy and utterly reliable so that you will be ready to fend off Satan's burning arrows of doubt, denial, and deceit and no longer be vulnerable to spiritual defeat.

Remember, too, that Satan battles for your mind, so keep focused on the Lord Jesus and the devil will never establish a stronghold in your thoughts. All that I have written is about defence but you have no need simply to remain passive and defensive in spiritual warfare. You have a powerful and effective weapon in your hands – like a two-edged sword – cutting and destructive. That weapon is God's unchanging, authoritative, and magnificent Word. Jesus used it against Satan to take absolute authority over him, and so can you.

One more thing – learn to pray supernaturally so that your mind will remain focused and clear; your emotions balanced and stable; your will firm and decisive; and your spirit fresh and vibrant in the flood-tide of God's life wherever you are and whatever you need. Please reflect on this and get a firm hold of it. Never lose your vigilance and always remember you are not alone, for others are in the same boat as you and need your prayers.

Oh, and a personal request – don't forget me! I have opportunities even here in prison under great pressure, duress and discomfort. Pray that I might have the right words and the right attitude to communicate to those here with me what you and I have discovered and are discovering about the sheer undeserved generosity and favour of God's agenda for all men and women everywhere. I am on foreign soil here but I am convinced that I represent the King of kings. I need your prayers so that I can confront error with truth and religion with reality.

I want everything to be plain and above-board and so Tychicus – how I value his friendship and respect his ministry – will answer all your questions and tell you everything you need to know. There's nothing casual about his visit to you. He is coming to give you accurate information and needed inspiration.

May all those who are associated with us who receive this letter have a wonderful sense of well-being and eagerly grasp the unconquerable benevolence; the unconditional favour; and the undefeated good-will of God the Father and the Lord Jesus Christ. May all those who are committed to be faithful to our Lord Jesus Christ – even if it means martyrdom – continue to know His sheer, undeserved, and lavish generosity.

THE GOD-LIFE
AND ITS JOY

Paul's Letter to the

Philippians

Paul's Letter to the

PHILIPPIANS

~ CHAPTER 1 ~

T HIS IS A JOINT LETTER from both Paul and Timothy. A whole generation separates us but Jesus Christ makes us inseparably one. We are – both of us – aware of the mercy and the majesty of God. We are aware of His mercy because all we are and all we have we certainly don't deserve; and we are aware of His majesty because all we do and everywhere we go is in direct, unquestioning, and uncomplaining obedience to His clear, simple, and unmistakable commands. We have given up our rights, our status, and our security, and have become wholly dependent on and responsive to God's Messiah, Jesus of Nazareth.

We are writing to those of you who have become the community of Christ in the historic city of Philippi, which is now the strategic gateway to Europe. You share with us the constant and deliberate attempt to listen to the commands of Christ and to carry them out. We realise that you are determined to live within your society and within the affairs of your exceptionally affluent community with every aspect of your lives dictated by the standards of Christ and not by the standards of those around you.

132

We are writing also to those who have vision for the future – those who carry spiritual responsibility; show spiritual maturity; and exercise spiritual authority among you; and those – along with them – who take practical steps; release practical resources; and demonstrate management skills to make their vision happen. You have clearly recognised and released these leaders to function effectively among you.

May the sheer undeserved generosity of God and the irrational, comprehensive well-being that comes from the close, warm and intimate relationship we have with God and His risen, eternal, history-invading Son be your experience as you read this letter.

I have known and heard so much about you since those early days, when we first met and established a Kingdom-bridgehead from the East to the West. As I reflect and remember I am profoundly grateful. There are no regrets; no disappointments; no shadows in our relationship. You are constantly on my prayer-list as I name you before the Lord. When I picture you in my mind and pray for you personally, and particularly in my heart, something deep within me stirs; bubbles up; and overflows – it is undiluted and irrepressible joy! It happens every time!!

I have concluded that the reason for this is that we deeply share the same passion that the God-news would be significantly and relevantly released into the sin-darkened, despairing, helpless hearts of ordinary men and women like us. You have never faltered; never stumbled; never let up since first I met you until this very day. Knowing that this is so from the past into the present, I know that the future will not disappoint me because your conversion was not some superficial ritual in which you gave your hearts to Jesus, but rather you had a radical and revolutionary experience of God's power and holiness. The Holy Spirit came to lead you right into the heart of God and that is where your new beginning began.

This is why I am rock-solid confident of your future because you caught such a vision of God in Jesus through the Spirit, and you were so radically changed that your old life no longer carries the appeal or the power that it once had. The day is coming when this unfinished reality will be finished glory as Jesus returns personally and visibly into the arena of history and we see Him as He really is and become like Him.

I am not apologising for writing in this way to you for this is no emotional, sentimental, nostalgic spasm. You are now part of my life. It makes no difference to me whether I am holed-up in this isolated freedom-denying, constantly-under-observation prison, or robustly out there in the hustings resisting every attempt to undermine and discredit the releasing and redemptive truth of God's good news in Jesus Christ, and arguing step by step that it makes sense. The big thing for me is that we are in this together. We are certainly singing off the same song-sheet. Whatever you may think or others might say. God knows that what I am writing is true – I feel a deep, special, God-designed love for you all.

Because of this I ask that your focus will be clearer; your longing after God will be stronger; and your grasp and understanding of Him will be deeper; so that instinctively you will appreciate His perfect will for your lives and live in such a way that His holiness will never be disappointed or offended by you. I want, more than anything else, that though people may criticise some of the things you do and some of the things you say, they will never be able to criticise the transparency and integrity of who you really are until, at last, what has been called that great, divine, far-off event happens and the reigning, triumphant, glorious Lord Jesus breaks into human history again for the second time.

I urgently and incessantly beg and plead with God that the overwhelmingly visible evidence of this invisible relationship which you have with Him, through the perfect and completed work of His Son Jesus the Messiah, will be undeniably seen – and God will get the credit for it!!

One of the reasons I am writing to you is because I know that life poses some unanswerable questions that often disturb and distress us –

and sometimes fill us with devastating doubt and destructive thoughts. Injustice, unfairness, pain, and persecution often hound us to despair. However, I assure you, my dear Christian family, that my situation here is far from being negative although you may be confused by it.

The reality is that the Kingdom life to which we are committed has taken vast strides forward, not in spite of but because I am where I am now, in prison. You see, none of the political, civil, or military authorities here are left in any doubt whatsoever that I am a prisoner, not because I am some kind of fanatical, religious freak, beguiled by fantasy, but because Jesus Christ is risen from the grave and is alive in His new resurrection body and I have a living personal, vibrant relationship with Him now through the Holy Spirit of the living God. This has radically changed and revolutionized my life. It is precisely because I am where I am – a prisoner – that the vast majority of the Christian family are now – unhindered by threat or punishment – engaged in testifying to the fact the our God reigns and Jesus Christ, His Son, is alive.

Of course I realise that not all who impact society with the good news of God's sheer, undeserved favour do so from pure motives. Some, quite bluntly, do so because they are jealous of the prominence I have gained because my well-known, formal, legalistic religion has been transformed into a living relationship with God, and they want that publicity and prominence for themselves.

However, not all by any means are like that. Many share Jesus with humility, honesty, and absolute integrity because of what He has done for them and because He is so real to them. They do this not only because they want to bless God and benefit others, but also because they are aware of my situation that, for the moment, silences me and they want to use their freedom to identify with me and to declare openly and clearly what burns within my heart.

Those who are jealous of me, and appear to want to compete with me, cloak their self-centred motives in piety, and at the same time seem to want to make things even more difficult for me, while I am unable to defend myself before others. But listen carefully to what I am writing to you – whatever causes people to share the goodness and unearned favour of God with others is irrelevant so far as I am concerned.

Outstripping everything else is the fact that many are hearing about who God is; what God is like; and what God has done in sending His Son into the world to rescue humanity and give every man, woman, boy, and girl the chance to respond to His love. I wrote at the beginning of this letter that when I think of you something stirs deep within me; bubbles up; and overflows in undiluted and irrepressible joy. That very same joy floods my whole being when I realise that although I am here in prison God's purposes are still being gloriously fulfilled.

Nothing will deter or diminish my joy because I know I am constantly on your prayer-list, and I am continually resourced by my Heavenly Father as He credits me with the risen life of His dear Son, Jesus, through the precious, unfailing ministry of the Holy Spirit. And so I know – not just in my head or my heart; not just through my understanding or my emotions; but deep, deep in the very core of my being – that God is in absolute control and I am part of His unfolding agenda. What an incredible wonder that though I am in chains, I am free.

Uncertainty always has a corrosive quality about it that eats into the deepest parts of the human heart, and I am aware that I am not immune to this. Yet, in facing this reality with all the pressure it brings upon me, I am still filled with an uncurtailed optimism and undeterred expectancy that I will not let my Saviour down, and I will be able to look you straight in the eye as I summon enough boldness to honour Jesus whether I live or die.

You see, so far as I am concerned, being here on earth is giving the risen Christ a place to live; and no longer being here on earth will be God giving me a place to live; and there is no contest when it comes to deciding which of these two is better. I have no doubt in my mind that were I to continue here on earth God would go on reproducing His life in and through me. So I am confronted with a huge dilemma.

Although I am usually thought to be a clear-thinking, decisive person indecision now grips me. I realise that ultimately it is not in my hands whether I live or die but, in my present situation, that does not prevent me from reflecting on what I would prefer and what would serve you better. This is quite painful for me, for with all my heart I long to leave the land of the dying and go to the land of the living where there is strength without weakness; service without weariness; living without sinning; and presence without absence yet I know that your development and maturing would be much better served if I remained on earth.

I have come to the conclusion that, because of this, my imprisonment will not end in death, but God will preserve my life so that I will still have input into your lives, helping you along your journey, and ensuring that following Jesus Christ will never be dull or boring for you. One day, I believe, I will be released and together we will experience the undiluted and overflowing joy-life. I hope it is all right with you that I share my innermost hopes and dreams in this way.

However, God is in absolute charge!! He knows the end from the beginning and the future is to Him as the past is to us. Please hear this voice from prison!! Live in such a way that the good news of God's grace in Jesus Christ will be endorsed in your life-style and enhanced by your demeanour. This will bless me more than you will ever know whether I am with you in person or simply hearing reports about you.

I will be assured that nothing will cause you to falter in the face of pressure because you are so inextricably bound together in the invisible and resilient bonds of Calvary love declaring and demonstrating in your unity that you have grasped the unseen but real world of eternity. How we need one another so that our fears and anxieties will be banished when we are confronted by those who want to bring us down. Without doubt this will serve notice to them that it is they and not you who will stumble and fall –

and that God has vindicated Himself in you. One of the accompaniments of true discipleship is experiencing the same hostility and pain Jesus knew as He lived as the God-man here on earth. As you know, I am speaking out of personal experience. So do not be discouraged or down-hearted in the midst of your pain for this is an ongoing reality that we all face.

∼CHAPTER 2∼

I feel so sure that you must be coming to know, as time goes by, more and more of that warm, intimate, secure relationship with Jesus; that immeasurable strength of His unconditional, pursuing love; that resilient, resourcing, risen life by His Spirit; that gentle, easy-to-be-entreated tenderness and deep, instinctive concern for others which He so consistently showed.

In the light of all of that – which I feel so sure must be so in your lives now – hear the cry of my heart so that the joy I feel towards you may be filled right up to the brim as you think as He thought and love as He loved, so that there would be no tensions; no disaffections; and no animosities among you either inwardly or outwardly.

Believe me when I say that I fully understand that all of us have a tendency to want to feather our own nest and behave often with empty arrogance – but, please, don't live that way! Instead, behave towards others in ways that are motivated by considering them better and more deserving than you are. Don't look around and compare yourselves with others but look within and challenge self-interest and self-indulgence. Don't act as judge and jury towards others when you have not walked in their shoes. Of course, you have needs, but so do other people and theirs as well as yours should be your concern.

A Christian life-style expressing and vindicating the reality of our salvation is such a huge, fundamental, and crucial issue among God's people that it requires huge, fundamental, and crucial attention. Soft talk, pious platitudes, and wishful thinking will not do. It will require the Jesus' life to be received and then to be released in you, through you, and among you. The Christian ethic will never really see the light of day without the Christian dynamic. It is not difficult to be a Christian – it is absolutely impossible! – apart from the vibrant, life-giving ministry of the Holy Spirit. It is only on that basis that I dare to use Jesus Christ as your realistic model.

Although Jesus had a previous life in eternity with God – talking to Him; mixing with Him; face-to-face with Him – because He was in essence and being God, it did not cross His mind for a single moment to cling to His indisputable divinity and His hard-for-us-to-understand-fully relationship within the Trinity of the Father, and the Son, and the Holy Spirit. In fact, as a somebody (indeed, the eternal, unique Somebody) He became a nobody when He was born as a baby, unspectacularly and unromantically, in an inhospitable out-house in Bethlehem.

He was exactly like any other baby in appearance and function. Not only did the divine become human and the eternal become historical in Jesus (which, in itself, is magnificent enough!) but this God-man became a slave, at the bottom of the social pile, with no rights, no possessions, no position, and no reputation. All who met Him, and came to know Him, never doubted His humanity. It was this man who gave up everything and claimed nothing who submitted to a worthless criminal's execution at the hands of the Roman authorities.

The execution which they had devised was, perhaps, the most barbarous and inhumane in all of human cruelty – a cross. God, the Father, reached down from the height of glorious and unique perfection in eternity to the profound and flawed depths of history and raised God, the Son, up through Resurrection and Ascension to the throne room of the universe and gave Him His pre-Incarnate name again – the Logos; the meaning and reason behind everything eternal and historical, seen and unseen.

It was this Name He gave up to become Jesus, the only Saviour of the world – and it is by this name that we recognise Him and relate to

Him. One day He will be seen and known for who He really is – the-meaning-and-reason-behind-everything Saviour of the world – and the only appropriate and instinctive response will be submission and surrender by angelic hosts, human multitudes and demonic hordes. All will be united in declaring who He really is – the Saviour-Messiah who is God – and, at last, the comprehensive and complete splendour of God, the Father, will be recognised.

Because of all this, my precious Christian family, please realise that if God does not work in you and through you, you can do nothing. Please realise, too, (oh, please be convinced and assured of this!) that if you do not give yourselves in fresh obedience and commitment to a life-style marked by humility and harmony with one another, God is severely restricted in doing anything of eternal worth and value.

Give yourselves to a totally new way of living because you are God-people now and it is completely and dangerously wrong to think of salvation only as a past encounter with Christ, for it is also a present experience and awareness of His living, reigning presence within you. Give yourselves to His salvation life-style with godly awe and life-impacting wonder. When I was with you I was so encouraged by your eager responsiveness to the revealed heart of God, but now that we are separated from one another it is even more important for you to live this way so that God can fulfil His agenda through you.

Let's put some 'flesh' on this. Whatever you do, do it gladly, enthusiastically, and eagerly without looking around for reasons why others should be living in the same way as you are – or even doing these things instead of you. This free, responsive, uncritical, willingness in you will help you on your journey towards being above reproach, transparently clean, and guileless which are indisputable marks of being born again by the Spirit of God into the family of God.

The culture and context in which you have to live out your lives is certainly not like that for it is twisted, tainted and bent and very much at the mercy of its animal instincts. As darkness increases around you it is all the more important that you are like lights shining in the darkness offering hope where there is despair; joy where there is sorrow; and fulfilment where there is frustration.

I want you to live and behave in this way so that when the Books are opened and the Records are revealed, after Jesus has returned to reign and is sitting on the Judgement Seat, I will be proud of you all and realise that every effort I made and every input I had into your lives was so worthwhile.

I want you to know that even if this is the end for me because of the accusation against me for proclaiming another King superior to the Emperor of Rome among you and others, I am deliriously happy because of the reality I have discovered in Christ and I see being worked out in your lives. So, lift up your heads; open up your hearts; and sing praise and thanksgiving to God with unhindered joy.

Sooner, rather than later – if the Lord Jesus allows it to be so – you will not only read what I have written but you will hear from Timothy – who has been such a blessing to me here – how things really are with me. Open your hearts to him so that his report from you to me will be such a wonderful encouragement. Timothy is a very special young man and so far as I am concerned no one could take his place. He is as deeply concerned for you, as I am, with a selfless integrity that is devoid of all personal ambition. That is a rare characteristic since human nature can take even the most sacred and holy things and try to turn them to its own advantage and so Jesus Christ is robbed of His glory.

I know that you know this about him as he comes to you. He is no fly-by-night opportunist for he has stayed the course through thick and thin as we have journeyed together in response to the call of God on our lives. So at the first possible opportunity he will be on his way to you. Indeed,

God willing, I am hugely optimistic that in the not-too-distant future I, too, will be there with you in person.

Epaphroditus, as you know, has had very serious health problems and although I appreciated, more than I could ever have expressed, your thoughtfulness and kindness in sending him to me, to take care of the practical issues here, I have had to persuade him to come back home to you. What a huge blessing he has been. His heart-fellowship and loyal comradeship, and his determined discipline in Kingdom warfare have been an enormous inspiration.

You sent the best to me when you sent him. However, ill-health has weakened him and home-sickness often overwhelms him as he realises your deep concern for his welfare. He certainly was desperately sick and I even wondered if he would survive. But God spared him and was so wonderfully gracious not only to him but to me in doing so. Things are bad enough here but Epaphroditus dying would have broken my heart. It will be such a relief to me when he returns home and I will then know that he is safe and secure with you.

You can look after him and help him to get fully fit once more in a way that I cannot do here. I know that you will receive him with open arms and give him the respect and honour that is due to those who stand looking into the abyss of death, because of their commitment to serve Jesus Christ whatever the cost. Discipleship is a risky business and certainly gives no guarantee so far as this life is concerned. He came to me in enthusiastic obedience to represent your love and care for me. I really wish I could put into words how much he has meant to me.

∼ CHAPTER 3 ∼

As I come to the end of this letter, my dear Christian family, I cannot stress enough that in the midst of all the ups and downs of life I want you to be filled with irrepressible joy whatever your circumstances. If I repeat myself it is not because my mind is wandering and I have lost my focus, but because I see dangers within and confusions without and I want to warn you about their disastrous implications.

Be on your guard against those who shamelessly pervert the amazing grace of God in Christ; those who cause others to move further away from God rather than draw them nearer to Him. They are on Satan's side because they want to rob people of reality and return them to being religious again. They want to insist on rules and regulations; do's and don'ts; rather than release them into the glorious freedom of a living, vibrant relationship with God through Jesus Christ our Lord.

As you know the outward marks of the Jewish religion were circumcision and keeping the Sabbath, but the evidences of a true relationship with God are not these outward signs but a life-transforming response of a supernatural submission and surrender to God – whatever that might mean in practical terms – even when it goes against common-sense. Human experience, human ability, and human wisdom have great value but when it comes to Kingdom stuff their value is limited and often these things are of no value at all.

It is so hard for us to come to terms with the reality that it is not what I do that counts, but what God does for me; in me; and through me – for Christianity begins and continues not with a big 'do' but with a big 'done'. We become Christians not with our hands but with our ears!! There can be few people who tried harder, did more, or went further than I did to please God – and it didn't work!

I hope it doesn't seem like boasting, but as I look back and compare myself with almost anyone else I would even dare to say that few, if any, could have been more circumstantially favoured in his religion and heredity than I was. I can match – and even go beyond – anyone else's background. I was born into a God-fearing, Law-observing Jewish family with an ancestry as pure as anything ever seen. At the appointed time and in the appropriate way I was marked as a Jew. I was an indisputable Hebrew from the most aristocratic tribe. I was fastidious and meticulous in keeping the Jewish Law. I demonstrated my commitment to Judaism by opposing with raw violence anything and anyone who contested and contradicted what I passionately believed. I never put a foot wrong when it came to Jewish rules and regulations.

For such a long time I was utterly convinced that my wholehearted devotion and unhindered dedication to my religious practices were impressing God and gaining His favour – and maybe some aspects of my character did benefit during this time – but now I look back and I am convinced how unprofitable and utterly useless it all was, now that the Christ-life has been born within me as a result of the sheer undeserved and unearned generosity of God. In fact I have come to the conclusion that every advantage I have enjoyed; every possession I have owned; every position I have occupied; every goal I have achieved; every reputation for godliness I have gained; are all less than nothing alongside the unrivalled and incomparable magnificence of the deep, embracing, intimate relationship I have with my Master, God's Saviour-Messiah.

Because of this overwhelming reality it has been my privilege to surrender everything I have ever had for the honour of His Name. It has not simply been a case of seeing all these human things that I coveted so much, as empty and valueless, but I have come to regard them as disgusting and offensive because they fed my arrogant heart and proud spirit and stood in the way of this vibrant reality that I have now found in Jesus.

I came, at last, to realise that no matter how hard I tried, and no matter how diligently I worked at my do's-and-don'ts religion, it never brought me into an unclouded and secure relationship with God. That spectacular reality is only possible by having a child-like confidence in who Jesus is and what He has done so perfectly. It can only be experienced as a gift to be gratefully and adoringly received and not as a prize to be laboriously and energetically won.

I cannot even begin to tell you how I long for an ever closer intimacy with God's Saviour-Messiah and experience the same power that raised Him from the dead in my physical body, that I am so aware of right now. I realise that this must never become some kind of vacuous triumphalism and that it will mean for me – as it meant for Him – misunderstanding, misrepresentation, criticism, betrayal, loneliness, and ultimately devastatingly dark condemnation. I am ready for that and even the shame, the ignominy, and the brutality of the death He died.

You see, I know that God transformed what so vividly seemed tragedy in history into triumph in eternity – for men said, "He is too bad to live!", but God said, "He is too good to die!" – and I would so much like to share in that death – defeating man's last enemy someday somehow.

I am far from knowing this reality that I long for in all its magnificent wonder. I am certainly so far from being like Jesus. However, I am also far from being discouraged or dissuaded and so I keep going, filled with hope and anticipation and expectancy holding firmly in my mind and spirit all that was in the heart of the Lord Jesus that I should become. My dear Christian family, I so realise that I am not there yet!!

Having said that (because it is true!) I want you to know that a single priority and a clear focus dominates all that I am: I have firmly and securely closed the door on my past and now my eyes are riveted on that yet-unreached horizon and every sinew and muscle that I possess is now concentrated on getting there. More deeply than you will ever know I realise that I am a sinner, broken by my arrogance and disobedience but restored by Jesus Christ in order to participate in good works that please God.

I am so overwhelmingly aware that I am not perfect; but Jesus Christ makes me righteous in God's eyes, and the Holy Spirit leads me to greater holiness. It was for this purpose that God created me and paid the full price to release me from being a prisoner to my pride, my passions, and my prejudices and it is for this purpose that I now live so that it can be achieved fully in my living – or even in my dying! When I get out of bed each day, I do so for one purpose: to love, obey, and serve God and His people. So it is onwards and upwards for me!!

I do not want you to think that I am somehow exceptional – not at all. I passionately believe that everyone who has left Christian babyhood behind them should have this focussed, driving desire vibrantly within him. If you disagree with this I know that no persuasion or pressure from me will alter your thinking – only God can do that; and He will! All I can say to you at this point is that wherever you are on your spiritual journey, be consistent and honourable to where you are, so that you do not say one thing and do another.

Because I am so convinced that I am what I am because of the completely underserved and unearned favour of God (it is so not of my doing!) my heart cries out to you, my precious Christian family, not only to read what I am writing and hear what I am saying, but to live as I am now living as so many are doing.

Pay close attention to the life-style of those who have chosen to live in the same way as us, for they have translated divine revelation into human response; doctrine into doing; and profession into practice. You have heard me say again and again – and I am terrified that familiarity will breed contempt – that many by their life-style contradict what Jesus made possible when He died for us on the Cross, and so they make an absolute nonsense of claiming a radically transformed life by faith in Him.

Because love and fear for you grips my heart I write to you in this way with this same warning, with an intensity that is difficult to contain: be careful of those who persuade themselves and others that they are allies of God's Kingdom when, in reality, they are enemies. Be in no doubt that their future is bleak and broken. They are completely dominated by transitory sensuality and they boast about a life-style which contradicts

Bible-informed godliness and displays raw humanism dressed up in spirituality.

Don't go down that road but realise we have different priorities and refuse to allow earthly possessions and passions to beguile you, for we belong to a different Kingdom which is eternal. It is on that reality that our eyes are fixed as we wait for the visible, personal return of the Lord Jesus into the arena of human history and the affairs of men in a coming Day, which will mean His presence after His absence; the shining of His glory after His humiliation; and the unveiling of His majesty and power after the concealing of His lowly birth at Bethlehem.

We know that this now-reigning Jesus who brought cosmos out of chaos will, on that Day, change our disease-prone, time-vulnerable, sin-beguiled human bodies into bodies that can only be compared to His resurrection body which enables Him to enjoy eternity right now.

∼ CHAPTER 4 ∼

In the light of all of this, my dear Christian family, I want only the best, the most, and the highest for you. Oh, how I miss you and have a homesickness in my heart to see you face to face for you fill me with irrepressible joy because you are the evidence of the undeserved favour of God at work in human lives and of how Christ has used me to bring you into this reality. It is because of this that I want you to distinguish the genuine from the bogus by observing life-style as well as words. Do not compromise one inch on your conviction that truth learned needs to be truth lived, otherwise it is not truth at all in Kingdom terms.

I have a special message for Euodia and Syntyche that they would put an end to their quarrelling with each other since both claim to be committed to and submissive to Jesus as Lord. My dear faithful partner in the Gospel, I am pleading with you to help these women to learn that fellowship is not based on agreement but on Jesus. Please get alongside them and minister this fundamental reality into their lives.

I am so bewildered by their behaviour because we were so closely involved together in Good News stuff, as were Clement and so many other colleagues who are known to God and whose names are written in the Book that God keeps, as having been transferred from the dominion of darkness to the Kingdom of God's dear Son. But I worry that where they were is not where they are – and that is not Kingdom living!

I am issuing a command so that you will respond with your will and not simply with your emotions: make a decision now to be joyful whatever your circumstances. Of course you cannot be joyful FOR every situation but you can be joyful IN every situation as you get a proper perspective – God's perspective. Whatever you situation never lose sight of the fact that your past has been pardoned; your present is provided for; and your future has a secure and unqualified prospect. So hear my command again: be joyful!!

You must demonstrate controlled strength wherever you are and whoever you are with, because the Lord is now in the saddle of your lives and the reins are securely and firmly in His hands. Stop worrying – this is a decision you must make whether you are the worrying kind or not, for worrying and praying cannot co-exist. Instead, with overwhelming gratitude, realise that your God's grace and power are such that nobody can ever ask too much of Him. The consequence of this is that God's incomprehensible peace will immunise your emotions and your thinking whether it is night or day. What a way to live! – for joy is peace dancing and peace is joy resting – but always joy and peace are our spiritual inheritance in Jesus.

To sum it all up, dear family, replace the false with the true, the tawdry with the noble, the wrong with the right, the dirty with the pure, the ugly with the lovely, the dishonourable with the honourable – in fact, replace everything that is sub-standard and inappropriate with the highest and the best – and let the most and the greatest alone be the focus of your attention. Everything I have taught you whatever the context – present or absent; spoken or written; formal or casual; privately or publicly – never let it go or compromise it. Again I say to you, imitate the life-style I have lived among you and you will not go far wrong. In fact the result will be that you will not only know the incomprehensible peace of God within you but you will also know the incomparable God of peace with you.

Thank you, thank you for the strong and yet tender ties that bind us together in Jesus, and for the tangible evidence of your understanding, compassion and care for me and your generosity towards me. Of course I have always known what has been in your hearts so far as I am concerned, but it is such a blessing to me that you have taken this opportunity to demonstrate your generous spirit.

I do not want you to think that I am saying this so that you would be under pressure to go on meeting my need in this way. I hope you will neither misunderstand me nor think me ungrateful, but I live life a day at a time and happily accept every situation that arises knowing that God will never fail me nor ever let me down. This is not passive resignation but active realisation.

There have been days when the larder has been empty and other days when it has been full; days when I have patted my contented stomach and other days when I have been on very short rations; days when paying the bills was no problem at all and other days when I wondered how I would meet my responsibilities. But through it all I have been careful, responsible and honourable – and I have never worried nor spent sleepless nights, because Jesus Christ within me by His Spirit has enabled me to live the God-life to the full – up or down; full or empty; secure or vulnerable. I can honestly say that nothing escapes His attention and so I can face whatever comes to me in life because He faithfully meets every need.

I am so anxious, in writing all this, to give you the impression that I neither need nor want your generosity. It is so difficult to express this without being misunderstood. It means more to me than I could ever express that you would know and share my life at every level. Cast your minds back to those days when you were brand new Christians and I had come from Macedonia to be among you, you might have expected – because of the beating heart of Christianity – that I would be well provided for but, in fact, I wasn't.

Those much more spiritually mature than you might have been expected to put their hands in their pockets and care for me, but they didn't. But you did and I was so affirmed, encouraged, and blessed by your meeting my need in Thessalonica. Please, please don't misunderstand me, I am not hinting to you to send money to me. Not at all! I am honestly and genuinely wanting that you would be blessed as you give, for there is a heavenly and eternal banking system at work that makes a nonsense of human accountancy. Generosity of mind, and heart, and hand lies at the core of Kingdom living. You can never outgive God!!!

I want you to know that my needs are more than fully met as a result of what you so generously sent me by Epaphroditus. I believe with all my heart that what you did not only met my needs but also met God's needs. Your generosity towards me blessed Him in an extraordinary way and brought great pleasure to Him. Be fully assured that this caring, compassionate God of ours knows our circumstances inside out and will never fail us physically, mentally, morally or spiritually. The evidence of this conviction lies in the fact of Jesus Christ – the best, the most, and the highest that He could give. Having given Him to us to be our Rescuer and Redeemer everything else, by comparison, is small and even paltry.

No wonder that though I am in big trouble here, I am deliriously happy and praise God, my Father, who has neither a beginning nor an ending with every fibre of my being.

Please assure all those with you there of my love, gratitude, and blessing. Those who are with me here join me in sending you their love and blessing. In fact the family of God in this great city know about your fellowship and kindness, and although they do not know that you feel the same bond of love in Jesus with them as you have with me, they send you their warmest greetings. Incredibly, right at the heart of government and in the corridors of power there are those who own no other king but Jesus our King, and they particularly wanted you to know of their love for you.

And now, goodbye, dear friends, and may you continue to know the sheer underserved generosity of God's heart, deep, deep down at the core of your being.

Paul and Timothy

THE GOD-LIFE
AND ITS FOCUS

Paul's Letter to the

Colossians

Paul's Letter to the

COLOSSIANS

MY NAME IS PAUL – no doubt you will have heard of me because of my close connection with Ephesus which is in your area, but we have never met. My personal history will not encourage you because of my intense and flagrant hatred and hostility towards the Church in years gone by. However, I had a powerful, life-transforming encounter with the risen Christ when I least expected it! Out of that encounter came a clear and unmistakable call and commission to be Christ's authorized representative to the Gentiles. Although I do not fully understand it I have been making the discovery that God does what He does, and that is what He did.

This letter comes also from Timothy who represents another generation from mine but, as you know, in the family of God age has little relevance. Timothy and I are related at a much deeper level than a blood-relationship.

It is because of this relationship – made possible by Jesus – that I dare to write to you so that you and I together might maintain and uphold Jesus' good reputation. This greeting is not formal but comes from my heart since I have learned so much about you from your father-in-the-faith, Epaphras.

154

I know that you have not only believed the incredible, good and revolutionizing truth incarnate in Jesus, but you are living in the reality that holiness is as important as forgiveness. I have heard so much about the context and environment in which you are living out your Christian lives there in Colossae, with its life-sapping, debilitating and confusing mixture of ideas and philosophies that have no particular code of doctrine.

My heart's desire is that you would experience and live in the overwhelming reality of God's sheer, undeserved generosity and His overflowing well-being towards you. As you know, this God of ours has no body – He is invisible; no birthdays – He is eternal; and no boundaries – for there is no restriction to His knowledge of us; to His presence with us; and to His power towards and through us. Wonder of wonders, Jesus taught us to call Him Father!!

Very few days pass without Timothy and I expressing our deep gratitude for you to this same Heavenly Father because, although we have never met, we have received such good reports about you. Particularly, we have rejoiced as we have heard of the reality and vibrancy of your redemption; the depth and strength of your relationships within the family of God; and the security and anticipation you have found in God's promises and provision when you leave this land of the dying and enter that land of the living.

Faith, love, and hope are three magnificent virtues dealing absolutely with our past, unbelievably enriching our present, and securing beyond our imagining our future. What Epaphras shared with you surely is good news rather than good advice, for it came to you with a resounding 'done' and not a demanding 'do'. Slowly, but nevertheless surely, this good news is being grasped and understood throughout the continents and is having the same transforming effect worldwide as it is having among you there in Colossae.

It is all about God's initiative and His sheer, undeserved generosity in all its reality. Epaphras is our source of information about you. What a man he is! He is a trusted colleague of ours too and increasingly has exercised a wider ministry which is of sterling value. It was from him that we learned about your positive and creative attitude and activities towards others which cannot be fully explained in human terms.

It is because of this that you are constantly on our prayer-list as we ask God to take you into His world so that you may serve His purposes in His way. We do this so that there will be unmistakable evidence of the invisible reality made vibrant by His Spirit within you . When all is said and done this is why we were created to be like Him; redeemed to enjoy Him; and filled with His Spirit to serve Him. You have made this wonderful discovery that God is not here for our sake alone, but we are here for His sake to give Him the opportunity to delight in us in private and in public; unseen and seen; in small things and in big things.

There is a spirituality which is mystical and a spirituality that is practical and benefits others – and both bless Him! He gives us not only the provision which will enable us to get to know Him better but also many opportunities to do just that. He does not leave us to struggle on our own but makes His own magnificent life available to us. It is because of this that we can keep going when others give up; persevere when others give in; and maintain an irrepressible gratitude to our Heavenly Father, who has given us a future and a hope that beggars our wildest imagination and our most romantic dreams. So our future has been secured; our freedom has been affirmed under the lordship of God's Son, Jesus; and our forgiveness is beyond doubt or dispute because of what that same Jesus has done.

O Colossians, you are in danger of losing sight of the fact that God has come near you. In former times God's people were warned not to try to portray Him with icons and images, but this is different. This is not man's insecurity or inventiveness but is God's initiative to come near and to dwell among us in His Son, Jesus. This Jesus has made the invisible visible; the intangible tangible; and the eternal historical – and He has done that in comprehensive perfection.

This has not diminished Him; lowered Him; or reduced Him. The reverse is true – He is over the created world; and forever before the created world. The created world is the result of His creativity – He made stars before stools; plants before ploughs; and trees before tables. He is responsible not only for the things we can see, hear, smell, touch, and taste but He powerfully controls those unseen powers that affect our lives here on earth, so practically and radically. He is the One who shapes the geography of the nations and controls the history of their people.

Absolutely nothing is beyond Him, over Him, or outside His grasp and authority. However far you can see; however high you can reach; however deep you can fathom – all came into being by Him; is held together in Him; and was made for Him. Never, never place Jesus alongside other spiritual beings – He is in a category of His own – unique, special, and distinctive.

So far as creation is concerned He brings life and so far as the Church is concerned He is Lord. For in the timelessness and endless space of eternity God the Father, God the Son, and God the Holy Spirit conferred together to create man to resemble them and so become capable of being God's family.

Alas, the family God created decided they knew better than God why they had been created and disregarded His instructions to them and so His image in them was distorted and they forfeited their relationship to Him. Human beings have chosen to do things their way ever since that beginning and have lived their lives adrift and alienated from God.

Some, however, recognized God's original intention; realised it was beyond human ability to do anything about it; rejoiced that God had a master-plan; repented of the stupidity; and received Jesus as Lord as well as Saviour. Now, on earth, there is a group of people who reflect Christ's supreme lordship – His Church.

God's master-plan is staggering, for He became man without ceasing to be God; He became creature without ceasing to be Creator; and having made the universe He came to live within it. His plan was to redeem what was lost; reconcile what was hostile; and mend what was broken. He did all that through His Son, Jesus. God who became man had to die in order to bring all things – not just people – to Himself. My mind cannot grasp it; my words cannot articulate it; my emotions cannot express it, that His precious eight pints of blood could bring back a whole universe to Himself!

But this I know, and to this my whole life is committed, that since Jesus died on Calvary's Cross, death is defeated, God's righteousness is satisfied, man's sin is forgiven, salvation for ordinary people can be eternally secure, evil has been conquered, freedom is now given to man to live a righteous life, hope is eternal, heaven is opened, the Spirit is released, wholeness is possible, and community on that basis is formed, over which Jesus Christ is Lord.

O dear Colossians, that's the theology; that's the theory; that's the truth. But you have entered into the reality of this incredible master-plan of God's and you have begun to experience its pulsating power – so the universal has become intrusively personal for you. There was a time when either through ignorance or through downright insubordination you were at war with God. You demonstrated this in the way you lived because of the way you thought.

But what a difference now; the whole situation has been reversed; God has taken the initiative. He has made you His friends even though your humanity, your frailty, your vulnerability lets you down from time to time. It is not that He condones or overlooks evil, but He has magnificently confronted it and dealt with it in His Son, Jesus, who actually, publicly, and painfully died by the Roman executioner's process.

As a result you can challenge the devil's lie and humanity's excuse, that nobody is perfect, for you can be blameless, flawless, and righteous before God because Jesus did what He did. You see God has offered you friendship so that fitness can result – not the other way round. However, I must issue a warning to you, if all that I have written is to be real for you and realised in you.

The Good News I brought you demands a personal response and a committed responsibility from you. The Good News from God makes something possible, but not inevitable. God has done His part but your part is to keep your eyes fixed and focused on Him, unwavering and determined, living the Jesus life in the power of the Holy Spirit, come what may.

A past response to the sheer, undeserved generosity of God does not cut the mustard. There must be the ongoing life of faith in the perfect, complete, and accepted work of Christ that affects every thought, every attitude, every word, every action, every intention, every reaction, every relationship, every motive that is part of your life every day. You see Jesus did not come to save you from hell and get you to heaven – He came to save you from your sins so that you can now live a righteous life.

You were not only saved from something; you were saved for something – the Jesus life; life under the government of God; Kingdom living. This is the hope that is aroused in the Good News of God. This is the heaven-sent message you have received and to which you have responded and for which I have surrendered my life and freedom.

God's calling on my life is to teach, strengthen, affirm, and encourage the new Body of Christ on earth – the Church. Jesus's suffering was unique, perfect, comprehensive, and complete. His atoning sacrifice on the Cross was once and for all – never to be repeated – for God's righteousness was satisfied there. However, there's a lot of suffering to be endured by His new Body on earth and that has been part of my job-description from God. I did not hear God call me under false pretences so I am content and can sing praise to God that I am shut up here in jail rather than you – for God not only reconciled me to Himself by the blood of His Son but He also recruited me for His eternal purposes; and you can't have one without the other!!

Jesus gave His life for me that I might live eternally and I gladly give my life for Him that He might live historically in me. My task – come what may – is not to tell you what I think or how I feel but to deliver to you the powerful, authoritative message of God without any limitation or restriction. It is incredible to me – with my Jewish background – that decade after decade of godly men and women sought after God for answers to the fundamental questions of life, but never quite broke through to understanding. But things are different now through repentance and faith in God's master-plan, focused in His Son, Jesus. The issue is not race but grace – that whoever you are Christ can live within you by His Holy Spirit. This is God's revelation to us and this is our hope of all the glorious things to come.

So, by one means or another we want you to know this incredible reality not only to bring people to faith but to help them continue and remain in that faith. Our concern is to confront and conquer the devil's lie that no one is perfect because God's secret is that in His Son you can be perfect before Him. It is for this that I strain every muscle and sinew not only physically but mentally, emotionally, and spiritually – and yet it is not me, really, but Christ at work in me and through me for I want to model what I am teaching.

~ CHAPTER 2 ~

It makes no difference to me that we have never seen one another face to face, for there is no effort I will not make; no territory I will not explore; no boundary I will not push; and no burden I will not carry on your behalf. Spiritually, mentally, and emotionally I want you to know that I am going flat out for your sake. This letter does not come as a result of polite courtesy but as an assurance of personal commitment both to you and to the family of God at Laodicea.

The thing that is driving me is a yearning that the depths of your emotions might be stirred, and the fibre of your wills might be strengthened in wanting only the most, the highest, and the best for one another, and that your minds might fully and overwhelmingly grasp the revealed master-plan of God, in sending the Rescuer and the Redeemer into history out of eternity.

It is in Him that you will see things clearly from God's point of view; and it is in Him that you are directly confronted with the unchangeable reality of what God is really like and what God has really done to bring light into man's darkness and hope into man's despair. Hear this, as clearly as I can say it and you can read it – Christ alone is all you need!!

I am writing to you in the starkest possible terms so that you will not be beguiled or mesmerised by the plausible words and subtle arguments of those around you. There are those among whom you live who want to add other elements to the Christian Faith, and I am terrified you will be seduced into mixing other Faiths with Christianity with the result that you end up with a religion. I want you to know that there is one thing the master-plan of God saves us from and that is religion. God wants to bring us into a vibrant relationship with Himself through His Son Jesus and save us from the rules and regulations of a man-achieved religion.

Although I am not there with you, I know what is going on; how easy it is to be misled; and end up with something which is not reality. Be assured that the absence of my physical presence in no way limits my involvement in the heavenlies on your behalf. I am overwhelmingly glad to know of your simple, uncomplicated, direct grasp of the unvarnished truth of the Good News of God and that your faith is built on nothing less than Jesus' blood and righteousness. It is on this solid rock – Christ – knowing that everything else is dangerous and deceptive quicksand.

I want so much that you would grasp firmly who it was you received when you were so powerfully born again through the mighty ministry of the Spirit of the living God. The Logos of eternity became the Saviour of

161

history; the Messiah promised through the ages came from God to bring mankind to God; the baby in the manger became the King on the throne, so that every day and in every way you would surrender and submit to Him.

He is the One in whom now you live and move and have your being. So, please, go on living in Him – allowing the roots of your being to grow down into Him giving you nourishment and strength and providing stability and security whatever life throws at you. Let the hidden, invisible relationship you have with Christ, however, become visible and unmistakable for all to see. What you have learned, live it out unashamedly and cause your gratitude to impress and impact those around you. Be warned that the devil will always want to make you dissatisfied with all that you have in Christ and try to turn your gratitude into grumbling.

Make absolutely sure that you have no truck with superficial and misleading philosophy that relies on the limits of the human mind and quickly would make you a prisoner to secularism and humanism.

Realise with the heady freedom of divine revelation that Jesus Christ is perfect in divinity; present in humanity; and powerful in authority. I beg you to see in a fresh way that in Him you forever have everything that you need.

You who are Jewish know that God wanted to mark those who are His by a physical act, but now Jew and Gentile alike participate in the unbreakable covenant of God, not through the blood of circumcision but through the blood of the Cross – and that requires your participation in consciously using your freedom to live a righteous, godly life.

You demonstrated and sealed this reality as you attended your own funeral service in baptism declaring that your old self had been crucified and that new, resurrection life is now pulsating through your veins, for the same power that raised Jesus from the dead is released and at work in your present, physical, earthly body.

You see, on the Cross Jesus suffered our death. Because of your sinful nature you were totally out of real communication with God – you were not speaking to Him and He was not speaking to you. This is the essence of death – communication is broken; separation is real; and relationship is absolutely gone. But it took almighty God to bring life out of death; fellowship out of separation; and communion out of conflict. Jesus did not deserve to die – His death was not a process; it was a penalty paid on our behalf.

This Jesus who deserved life had to go through your death to give you resurrection life. Never, never restrict or minimise what God has done in and through His Son, Jesus. Not only did He suffer your death on the Cross but He also settled your debts there. Debt cannot be ignored or forgotten. Someone has to foot the bill. Not everyone is in debt to men, but every one of us, without exception, is in debt to God. But Jesus took your legalistic debt to God and got you out of the red with God, by becoming poor with your poverty so that you could become rich with His riches by dying on the Cross.

Oh Colossians, wonder upon wonder, Jesus not only suffered your death on the Cross and settled your debts on the Cross, but He also secured your deliverance on the Cross. The spectacle of Calvary is not a good man dying for his cause or giving us an example of the consequences of being true to his convictions. On the Cross we see a man fighting every dark, supernatural force – and that is why the sky went dark on that first Good Friday. Jesus snatched away the weapons of the demons of darkness and so forever broke their power. But not only did He disarm them, He publicly disgraced them so that now they could be plainly seen for what they are.

In the light of all this magnificent reality do not submit to the criticism and condemnation of those around you because you do not observe two things, which have somehow or other crept into local Christianity which are essentially not Christian – special diets and special days. Christianity is not about legalistic taboos or external, restrictive observances; it is about living consistently in Christ every day and in every way. Why settle for the symbol when you can be enjoying and experiencing the real thing?

Be very careful of those whose sincerity is questionable because they claim to have a deeper spirituality as they make a parade of what they claim to have seen. As a result you could be in danger of being robbed of what God wants you to have. I beg you to watch out for those whose spirituality is limited. It is absolutely true that God is greater than the universe because He created it, but He is also closer than your breathing. There are those around you who try to resolve this paradox by mental gymnastics that go a long way to satisfying the intellect but ruin direct relationship with God through Christ. A body cannot live without its head. In the same way neither can you really live as part of the new Body of Christ on earth without a vital connection to the Head – Christ. So beware of spurious religion and meaningless ritual taking the place of a wonderful relationship and a vibrant reality that you undoubtedly have in Jesus Christ.

If you really were crucified with Christ, so that it is no longer you living but Christ living in and through you, why would you go on living as if this had never happened? Why would you give any room to man-made regulations that are fundamentally transitory. They can appear to be so permanent and plausible and appeal to our insatiable desire to earn God's favour, but are useless in practical terms. They can never deliver what they appear to offer!! Hear the sustained cry of my heart that you would have nothing to do with that stuff.

∼CHAPTER 3 ∼

Having died with Christ you are now living in Christ triumphantly and gloriously. Keep your focus on the throne-room of the universe where the King of kings reigns. Resist the huge and insidious temptation to think earth rather than heaven. The old you has gone and the new you-in-Jesus is alive and well. This is your now-life but your still-to-come-life is even more startling – the King is coming and the new heaven and the new earth will be your spiritual inheritance as you experience it with your new body.

Theology has to be translated into experience and what you believe has to be transformed into how you behave. Give no quarter to any evidence that you are dominated by earth rather than heaven, because what you tolerate dominates. Your sexuality has to be controlled not gratified; your passion for the wrong things has to be executed; and your ruthless self-seeking has to be destroyed and dismissed from the throne of your life. God will not continue to withhold His thunderbolt of displeasure forever – so be warned!!

It was bad enough to behave in these ways before you were transformed and regenerated by the living Christ, but now it is completely unacceptable, intolerable and reprehensible. The list goes on; for God not only sets His face against sexual and sensual sins, but also against social sins – long-lasting and slow-burning anger that wilfully and stubbornly refuses any attempt to reason with it or calm it down; the sudden, flaring, disturbing temper that, though quickly kindled, quickly dies but only after damage has been done; the viciousness of the mind that pervades everything with evil; the insulting, barbed way of speaking that is calculated to hurt lives and damage reputations; the obscene, coarse language that believes that it is smart and sophisticated but leaves a foul atmosphere behind it; the deliberate half-truth that is blatantly intended to mislead or to misrepresent.

All of these things need to be confronted and dealt with in the area of your will; your decision-making process. This is your responsibility to be in control of your life. The negatives need to be dealt with rigorously and the positives embraced so that there is evidence of your new life in God where heaven rather than earth dominates. The barriers of birth and nationality; ceremonial and ritual; culture and education; class and money are all comprehensively destroyed in Christ.

So, stand on your own two feet as God's eternally selected, clearly different, and greatly cherished people and demonstrate a heart of pity. Be known as those who are easy to live with. Let God do whatever He needs to do in you. Consciously put the reins of your life into God's hands. Never become cynical or despairing with those around you who are foolish and unteachable. Do not become bitter and retaliate when people insult you and treat you badly. Instead of behaving in these ways realise afresh that it is only in going on forgiving that you will be forgiven. Above and beyond everything else, clothe yourselves with unconquerable benevolence; undefeated good-will; Holy Spirit-engendered, Cross-demonstrated love, for that alone will bring the miracle of reconciliation and relationship among you as God intended.

When you lose peace in your heart and restlessness and anxiety replace it, stop what you are doing and retrace your steps to the place where your peace disappeared. You see, peace is like the referee's whistle in the hands of Christ – when peace goes the 'game' has to stop because something has gone wrong and needs to be dealt with.

Be assured, peace comes when you stop resisting the will of God in your life. He is always in control. This is how you were meant to live among people and before God. Let gratitude be the hall-mark of your living from morning till night. Loyalty to Christ our risen Saviour and enthroned Lord calls for total submission to Scripture and anyone or any church declining to believe and do what is written there, or failing in practice to be faithful to it, is to that extent a rebel against Christ.

Let your singing be an expression of your relationship with God and your response to God – gratefully and gladly submitting to Him. To make sure that everything is covered and I haven't left anything out – whatever you do; commending or condemning; consoling or challenging; rising or resting; working or playing; active or passive; important or trivial; laughing or crying – do it as if Jesus Himself were doing it through you, because God the Father through God the Son by God the Holy Spirit has made it abundantly possible for you to live this way. Hallelujah!

I want you to understand that God not only wants you to have rich resources but also to have right relationships. All these thrilling things I have been sharing with you must impact the way you live your daily lives. I want to speak to you about this as simply and as directly as I can so that there is no possibility of misunderstanding.

It will always be true that the strength of a nation is derived from the integrity of its homes, but I want you to know that the reality of salvation will also be demonstrated by God's order in the home. The revealed heart of God is not about the rights of husbands, wives and even children but about their responsibilities. Each has different responsibilities but that does not imply difference in value and status.

God's plan in marriage is that leadership is the responsibility of the husband and God requires that wives submit to their husbands. This is neither negative nor destructive because conscious submission leads to unconscious growth, fulfilment, and fruitfulness – simply because this is God's way. You need to know that any form of submission in the Christian life demands trust in God and complete faith in His plan – and wives who live this way bring enormous pleasure to Him. Husbands, too, have responsibilities for God assumes that you understand that a husband and wife are not two people anymore – each with his and her own rights – but they are now one person each with different responsibilities.

Your responsibility, husbands, is to have a deliberate conviction in your mind that will demonstrate itself in a deliberate policy of your life to seek nothing less than the highest good for your wife. You see, it takes all of a man to achieve Christian love – the love that Jesus demonstrated on the Cross, and is only a possibility by the enabling of the Holy Spirit. This will dismiss any ill-will you may have against your wife because of something she did or, indeed, did not do. Loving in this way is not patronising but is practical.

Children who are still within the care of the family and the protection of the household have a responsibility too – to be obedient. This is comprehensive obedience and it brings delight to Jesus not because your parents are always right but because this is right in God's order.

In this context of parent and child, fathers have a huge responsibility to exercise discipline with explanation and fairness so that it will be ultimately received as an expression of love and responsibility and not the result of anger, selfishness, or inconvenience. The result will be security, confidence, and hope.

And, finally, in this social environment, with its many relationships, you who are slaves, whether within a household or outside the home, have a responsibility to be respectful in your obedience, conscientious in your service and God-fearing in all that you do. You must do your work in this way because you know that you are being constantly regarded by God and one day you will be rewarded by God Himself. Leave the injustices and the unfairnesses that occur, in the hands of Jesus. He will undoubtedly sort it all out.

In the light of all of this, those of you who own slaves better behave in a righteous and responsible way, because you will give an account one day for how you behaved when you had the opportunity to do what is right before God.

~ CHAPTER 4 ~

Make prayer a priority in your lives giving time and energy to your fellowship with God. Always be alert for fear that the enemy of your souls might sneak up on you unawares and establish a foothold to his advantage within you. Among all the many blessings with which God has enriched you, ask Him for one more – the blessing of a grateful heart.

Release us in your prayers into the purposes of God for our lives so that we might grasp the opportunities God gives us to declare the unveiled secret of God's heart that He was in His Son, Jesus, reconciling the world to Himself. What we are talking about here is not our hobby or our pastime to be lifted and laid when it suits us, for it is because of this magnificent reality that I am where I am today paying the price of faithfulness to the revealed truth of God. Ask God to help me to make His Word fruitful and to enable me to be a witness who is faithful.

Live in such a way before not-yet Christians that you are guided by how God sees them and not by how they appear to you. Be aware of circumstances where you know it is the right time to share the truth and the reality by which you live. When you speak do it with courtesy, sensitivity, and appropriateness but always with God-based hope like fertilizer, promoting growth from the soil and with God-revealed warning, like disinfectant killing all that is destructive and deadly. It is never easy to have the right response in every situation for sometimes we can be so truthful that we are not gracious and sometimes we can be so gracious that we are not truthful. Remember grace and truth came by Jesus Christ and He is alive within you by the Holy Spirit.

Tychicus will have all the information you want about me. What a man he is – tender and secure in relationship; constant and consistent in service; and along with us submitted and surrendered before the Lord. He is coming to you so that you will know exactly how things are here and you will not be discouraged and saddened because of lack of information or even by misinformation.

His travelling companion is Onesimus whom you know so well because of his relationship to you. I have so valued his fidelity to God and his loyalty to me. Between them you will be given a very clear picture of our situation.

Aristarchus, my constant companion in jail, wants to be associated with me in our concern for you, as does Mark, the kinsman of Barnabas (incidentally, whatever you have heard about him I want you to receive him with open arms). Jesus, who is better known as Justus, wants to be included, too, in this list of fellow-workers. These men have a similar religious background to me and have been such an encouragement and strength in this incredible privilege and responsibility of declaring and demonstrating that God's reign has already begun in His Son, Jesus.

Epaphras, too, whom you know well as a man committed to allow Jesus to accomplish His purposes through him, also sends his greetings. I have watched him constantly and personally praying for you with great fervour. These are not vague, general prayers but are focused on your constancy to fulfil all that God wants to accomplish in you and through you – that you will neither be superficial nor uncertain as you go about His business. I have no hesitation in assuring you that he offers himself wholeheartedly as part of the answer to his own praying not only for you but for those also in Laodicea and Hierapolis.

Luke, who is so knowledgeable and helpful with his medical advice, and is so special to you and me, along with Demas, who has been so fully restored, want to be remembered to you. Oh, and before I forget, in the midst of all these people I would be so grateful if you would remember, on my behalf, to greet the God-family at Laodicea and Nympha whose generosity and hospitality is so well known by our brothers and sisters in Christ there.

This letter contains so much concern over the life-sapping, debilitating, and confusing mixture of ideas and philosophies that have no particular code of doctrine and definitely distort your focus on Jesus, that I want it to be read to our brothers and sisters in Laodicea. It would also be important that you read their letter.

Before I finish this letter I have just remembered that I wanted to ask you to give this message to Archippus – do not give up too easily or give in too quickly to the pressure you are experiencing in the Lord's work. Having begun so well make sure that you finish what God has given you to do.

Although it is neither easy nor comfortable – because I am chained to a Roman guardsman – I wanted you to notice that this letter is so important to me that I did not want to dictate it but to write it myself.

May the sheer, undeserved generosity of the heart of God be your constant experience.

Paul (and Timothy).

THE GOD-LIFE
AND ITS HOPE

Paul's First Letter to the

Thessalonians

Paul's Letter to the

THESSALONIANS

~

T HIS IS A LETTER FROM PAUL, Silas, and Timothy to the believers in
Thessalonica whose lives are committed to and lived for God (no
longer distant and remote, but close, and intimate, and warm because Jesus
taught you to call Him Father) and His divine-become-human, long-
awaited and anointed Son.

May you know and experience God's sheer, undeserved, and lavish
blessing, and His joy-giving confidence.

As we write to you now we would want you to know how much you
mean to us and how profoundly grateful we are to God for you. It is not
possible for you to be aware of this depth of feeling we have for you, but
God knows our hearts as we pour them out constantly before Him. As we
think of you and pray for you we are inescapably reminded of these three
great Christian virtues – faith, love, and hope – which you so plainly and
powerfully demonstrate. The sterling service you render is clearly not the
result of human endeavour and enthusiasm but the direct consequence of

your total dependence upon God, as you allow Him to be who He is in you and through you.

Your hard work, which is obvious to everyone, is motivated and driven by Calvary-like compassion, and a desire to demonstrate that only the very best is good enough for God. Your ability to keep going when others have given up is obviously the result of knowing that the One who died in shame and ignominy will return in power and great glory, giving you new bodies like His and establishing forever a new heaven and a new earth. This is what stimulates our admiration of you and our prayers for you.

We have complete assurance, dearest family – cherished by us and, undoubtedly, the object of God's affection – that you are not an after-thought, you are a forethought in the mind and heart and purposes of God. You are not there in Thessalonica by chance but by choice. God had a plan for your lives – individually and congregationally – before Pentecost; before Calvary; before Bethlehem; and even before the Garden of Eden. In fact you were in His heart in eternity.

The evidence of this, so far as we are concerned, goes back to our first contacts with you. The unhindered, limitless Good News that we brought to you was not just talk, it was truth, overwhelmingly anointed by the Holy Spirit and affirmed and demonstrated by a life-transforming reality that came from the deepest depths of our being. As a result, we so clearly saw – and continue to see – that the Spirit of God uses the Word of God to enable ordinary people to become like the Son of God before our very eyes.

It isn't a secret that you saw this reality modelled in us so that what we said was, in fact, what we were. Belief and behaviour were consistently matched up. With this blue-print of Christ-likeness before you, you launched into this vibrant reality for yourselves and you began to be gloriously changed. Although pressured on every side you grasped with both hands what we said and discovered a supernatural joy that no human circumstances could ever impart to you.

This was such a powerful, transforming reality that you, as a church, not only became the talk-of-the-town but a challenging target for the whole region and indeed the nation to aim for. In fact what God was doing among you breached every human border so that without restriction the God-life was seen to be real in places and by people you have not even heard of. You will never really know how much we have been strengthened, affirmed, and encouraged by what has happened among you.

It is equally widely known that it all began as a result of the Good News of God we brought to you and how you wholeheartedly and without reservation or inhibition responded to it. Until that time everyone knew how things were with you. You were overwhelmed and totally committed to the images of the gods you had created in your own minds and fashioned with your own hands. You certainly were religious but there was no reality there. You had to be satisfied with what you had created rather than with the Creator who always was; who always is; and who always will be.

Then you encountered this always-is God and a living relationship and vibrant reality took the place of dead religion and useless routines. Truth broke through the terror of the unknown. God gave you a future and a hope that is based on His death-conquering, grave-shattering, darkness-banishing Son, who will personally and visibly return into the arena of history and the affairs of men assuring us of His presence after His absence; unveiling the shining of His glory after His humiliation; revealing His majesty and power after the concealing of His lowly birth at Bethlehem; and delivering us from the terrifying, eternal consequences of sin.

⮂ CHAPTER 2 ⮀

Our dear family, we are convinced – and we like to believe that you are too – that when we met with you it was a significant and strategic time. One of the beguiling misrepresentations which bedevils the Christian is that the God-life is easy and leads invariably to a path strewn with roses. Nothing could be further from the truth because Jesus assures His disciples that in this world they will face big trouble. When a storm breaks over us we can so easily conclude that what we are involved in is a mistake – we got it wrong; we are chasing a rainbow; we failed somehow.

In this regard you have already heard through our testimony of what happened to us at Philippi – the pressure we were put under; the pain we experienced; the slander and misrepresentation we encountered and endured. However, we never held back from telling you the whole story. We were utterly and absolutely convinced, in spite of all that went on to discourage and, indeed, to try and destroy us, that the vibrant, life-giving Good News of God's sheer undeserved favour and generosity towards us may well provoke strong, seductive, and slanderous resistance and resentment but it remains what it undoubtedly is – life-transforming, radically intrusive, God-honouring truth.

It is because of this we were bold enough, with God's enabling, to share this truth with you regardless of all that had been happening around us to discourage and deter us. We never attempted to pull a fast one on you by distorting the truth or working to an ungodly and devious agenda. The very reverse of that is the truth – we came to you with a message born in eternity and authenticated in history, as messengers called and anointed by God.

One thing is for sure that one day we will answer to Jesus before His Judgment Seat after our resurrection with our new bodies, for what we have said; what we have done; and where we have gone. He is the One who not only will pass judgment on us then, but who knows the motives and intentions of our hearts now. He certainly knows what Master we were attempting to serve when we came to you. Hopefully, you are aware that as we lived among you and shared with you we were men of complete openness, transparency, and integrity. Neither in the way we spoke to you nor in the things we did among you was there ever a selfish or acquisitive agenda running. Of course, God alone is the One who can realistically pass a verdict on this – our driving, relentless desire and focus was always to bring blessing and pleasure to Him rather than bask in the commendation and approval of men.

As those sent out by Jesus Christ, we could so easily have put pressure on you because of our certainty of our calling and our burning urgency to get you to understand and respond to the message we brought. However, as you know, that was not the climate of our relationship with you. Indeed, the whole atmosphere when we were together could only be described as maternal tenderness. We so desperately wanted the best, the most, the highest for you that we were neither content nor satisfied simply to tell you God's Master-Plan in His Son, Jesus, but we wanted to give ourselves to you without pretence or reservation.

You really got right into our hearts and became so deeply precious to us. These great days are not so far away in the past that you could have forgotten that clearly we were not 'on the make' among you but that we took every opportunity – however demanding, exhausting, and burdensome it was with the long, hot days and the even longer wearying nights – to provide for ourselves without any expectations from you, so that neither you nor anyone else would suspect any selfish or ulterior motive as we shared God's Master-Plan in Jesus with you.

You observed, as God did, our integrity, our purity, and our godliness while we lived out our lives among you. Our ministry among you was never remote or distant, or aloof. In fact it was quite the reverse of that – it was personal, individual, and intimate like a parent with his child. Our constant and unwavering concern was always that what you knew and understood would be translated into behaving in such a way that God would be honoured. He is the One who invited and welcomed you under His kingly and compassionate rule and protection, so that you could share in His limitless fullness and splendour. That is why we affirmed you when you were discouraged; came alongside you when your strength was flagging; and persisted in challenging you to the highest and the best.

178

Another thing which caused us so much joy and constantly made us praise God was the clear evidence that you appreciated and understood that what we shared with you was not our opinion, our idea, or our conclusion but what it really was – the revelation of unchanging and unchangeable truth out of the heart of God. You knew that because when our message was ignited by the Spirit of God, things began to happen within you and through you. In addition to that there were obvious similarities between you and the Judean communities of faith because the Jesus-life shone through you in the same way as it did through them.

Also, on the darker side, you became victims of the same pain, pressure, and persecution from the least likely source – your own people – as they did. Let me remind you that these same people were the very ones who took God-made-flesh, our dear Saviour, Jesus, and put Him to death. They also silenced forever those who supernaturally knew God's thoughts; were aware of God's agenda; and felt God's heart-beat. They made it abundantly clear that they would have no truck with us whatsoever.

You need to know, too, that they caused God to be angry because they were utterly exclusive in their religion, denying hope and a future to any who were not of their race. This is why they so bitterly opposed us as we shared God's undeserved favour and generosity with non-Jews so that they, too, would have the opportunity to come into God's family as His adopted sons and daughters.

This is the tragedy of Judaism, that refusing God's Master-Plan of salvation for themselves they try to prevent others from experiencing and enjoying what God has so gloriously provided through His Son, Jesus. Such a selfish, exclusive, and arrogant attitude and activity is deeply offensive and completely unacceptable to God and causes His unlimited anger to be poured out upon them.

Oh, our dear Christian family, this is why we are writing to you with such pathos and concern, because we wanted you to be left in no doubt that when we were severed from you for a season (in body but never in heart!) we left no stone unturned to get back to be with you. This was our profound and heart-felt desire. All of us felt exactly the same way. I, Paul, particularly tried repeatedly to get to you – but Satan put a road-block in the way and made it absolutely impossible.

Although Satan has frustrated and hindered our fellowship here on earth there is a time coming when neither he nor anyone else will be able to interfere with what God always intended – unrestricted and deep relationships with one another. Be assured, the King is coming, robed in glory unsurpassed, when every human being will behold Him and mankind's history will cease. On that unique and inexpressible Day you will be there – unmistakable evidence of what God has done for you; been in you; and given to you out of the sheer, undeserved generosity of His heart.

Believe me when I say that that is what we look forward to; that is what brings us unhindered exhilaration; that is our prize and reward for our mission accomplished and our ministry fulfilled among you. When we gather in His presence to share in the magnificent drama of worship before Him, that will be one of the chief reasons for our unbounded joy and gratitude.

∽CHAPTER 3∽

When separation from you became unbearable, we came to the conclusion that because of the intellectual pressure and exposure to ridicule – as well as a minimal measure of encouragement – we were experiencing in Athens, it would be better that Silas and I remained there on our own and we would send Timothy to you to make sure you were standing firm in spite of all you were going through.

We cannot speak highly enough of Timothy – our close colleague who shares our spiritual heart-beat and God-impregnated-DNA. We wanted him to bring resilience and unbounded optimism to you in your walk with God so that no pressure or confusion would cause you to falter. It is no secret that the road of pain and suffering is the one that we have been called upon to walk as the disciples of Jesus Christ.

No doubt you will remember, in our many conversations together, that we were constantly saying that this would be our lot. Our intention was never to be melodramatic or extreme for, as you now know, so it has turned out to be for you as for us. We did not hear from you and my anxiety became intolerable for no news is not always good news. It was because of this that I acted as I did so that I could have a first-hand account of how things really were with you.

I preached the God-News among you and you received it not because it is nice but because it is true. However, I know only too well that when you embrace truth and reality you will immediately come into conflict with error and falsehood. That really scared me because I know that the devil is not only strong but he is also subtle. I was frightened that all the good things we shared together would be totally lost.

It will be difficult for you to understand how absolutely thrilled we are to have Timothy back with us, having spent time with you, telling us that you continue to have absolute dependence on and trust in God and a deep commitment to want the highest, the best, and the most for one another. It was an overwhelming joy to us to know that you remember our time together in past days with pleasure and affection and that the yearning to meet up together in future days is mutual.

As a consequence, dearest friends, the anxiety and pain we are experiencing for the sake of the truth God so clearly and firmly put into our hearts and lives, is enormously eased by Timothy's report. You have caused the transforming vitality of God to flow again in our veins as we have heard that your faith that acts, and your love which cares, has never wavered. God alone knows and understands our profound and limitless gratitude and joy for all you mean to us. You are certainly on our prayer-list and never a moment passes without our asking God to make it possible for our fellowship to be renewed, so that you will have all that God wants you to have and any gaps in your faith will be filled.

We want our re-union with you to be a God-thing, with both our Heavenly Father and His reigning Son involved in the event. May that pure, selfless, sacrificial love which Jesus so powerfully demonstrated on the Cross at Calvary and which, apart from the Holy Spirit within us, is impossible for us to express, overwhelm you and be more and more the hallmark of your relationships with one another and towards those who have any contact with you. That alone defines and conveys what is in our hearts for you.

The Day is coming when God-made-flesh-in-history who, after His Resurrection, ascended to be God-now-reigning in the throne-room of the universe, will undoubtedly come back on earth. That Day will be sudden and decisive and He will be visible, personal, glorious, and powerful. It will wind up this present Age and the dead will be resurrected.

Angels will accompany Him and believers who are still alive on earth at that time will rise up to meet Him in the air. Our prayer for you in the light of all this incredible, cosmic reality – the climax of human history – is that you will be assured and unashamed as you enter into the flawless perfection of the unlimited fullness of the only God who really exists. It is with this in mind that we pray that you will experience and express the God-life now.

∼ CHAPTER 4 ∼

As we come towards the end of this letter, dearest family, we wanted to remind you of the practical teaching we gave you about the principles and practice of the God-life – and clearly, from what we hear, you have taken what we taught to heart. We are writing to you now so that you will not only keep going but increase and extend your faithful living of the God-life. You will remember that the teaching and truth we shared with you had nothing to do with our opinions, or our ideas, or our prejudices – it had God's seal of authority and approval from His Messiah-Son, Jesus.

You see, holiness is positive rather than negative – it is not just about not-doing but much, much more about doing. Holiness is certainly not about removing ourselves from people it is rather about relationships with people. People are often concerned about the will of God for them. Frankly they do not need to look any further than this – holiness is God's will for them.

In this regard, one of the most basic areas of living and so one of the strongest driving forces in every human being is our sexuality. We realise that there are huge pressures and problems, not only within you but also all around you – the Jews, the Greeks, and the Romans disregard their marriage vows and divorce among them is disastrously easy. Both personally and socially you are confronted by enormous challenges.

Let me put it as simply and clearly as I can – holiness must operate in your sexuality. The question you must answer with integrity is this – does your sexuality control you or are you in control of your sexuality? It is so easy to confuse – and so excuse – lust with love. Be assured that loyalty needs to be put into love and responsibility needs to be put into every relationship. We are certainly not just higher animals; we are a special God-creation. This gives us distinctiveness and dignity.

As a result of this, God will not stand idly by when we flagrantly turn a blind eye to His instructions and we blatantly use people for our own pleasure. We affirmed this when we were with you and cautioned you then about disregarding God's clear and unmistakeable way. God has called us to obedience, to self-control, and to purity. Be very careful, then, for fear that you slight the Holy Spirit who not only conveys the truth to us but enables us to live it.

Of course you know perfectly well that anyone who thinks he is holy but doesn't love his fellow-Christian is deluded. Holy living that is authentic is always filled with warmth, and love, and affection. Holiness, then, is not only to be selfless, responsible, and self-controlled sexually but also spiritually in your deep, transforming relationships with other Christians. You can never be holy by yourself – it is impossible to be holy without relating to other Christians.

Christianity is always personal but it is never private. We must come to Christ singly but we can never live in Christ separately. It may well seem unnecessary to write to you about this because it seems that your relationships there in Thessalonica are a by-word for warmth, for tenderness, and for compassion, not only in your own community but throughout the whole country. The reason we are pressing you in this is because you can never get too much of a good thing spiritually.

We felt it right, too, to highlight the importance of three things as you live out the God-life in that non-Christian environment where you are. The first of these is calmness and contentment. You see, holiness will always be unobtrusive and will quietly get on with the job. It never draws attention to itself by becoming exhibitionist, hysterical, excitable, or silly. Fanaticism is more dangerous to the Church than persecution, for persecution with all its injustice, pain, and bewilderment refines and purifies the Church whereas fanaticism discredits, disrupts, and ultimately destroys it.

If the first thing to characterize your God-living in a godless environment is calmness and contentment, the second should be our concern for personal consistency. The person who is holy must be more concerned about his own personal behaviour than about the behaviour of others. To be holy is not to become a busybody – interfering with the behaviour of others; intruding into their affairs; and meddling in their lives. It is a big enough challenge to live consistently ourselves!

The third characteristic of holy living in a godless environment is conscientiousness. The reality that Jesus is coming back to this planet is never a reason for stopping work – rather it should be a reason for working harder than we have ever worked before. To become super-spiritual, indolent, and a non-contributing member of society is to bring Christianity into disrepute. So have no truck with layabouts; spongers; social parasites who get absorbed and side-tracked in endless religious discussions.

You are well aware that the non-Christian world doesn't see you in church – worshipping, learning, and praying – but they do see you in their world. In fact this is the only part of your Christianity that they can see. Holiness is not something you do outside working hours. The simple fact of the matter is that your working life provides you with the opportunity for holiness.

Without doubt the greatest incentive of all to living a holy life in down-to-earth, practical living is the fact that our Lord Jesus Christ will come again out of eternity into history and out of heaven onto earth. This, unquestionably, is the next great world event. It will mark the end of one era and the spectacular and unique dawning of another.

Dearest friends, I realise you are anxious about those fellow-believers who have died before this historic, cataclysmic event, because you are afraid that they will miss out in some way. The pagan world around you certainly affirms that where there is life there is hope, but we affirm to you, on the authority of the Lord Jesus, that where there is death there is hope for the Believer. The pagan pressure around you could cause you to despair when you face the reality of death, but we have tremendous news for you – the Christian dying is to the spirit, what going to sleep is to the body. In that sense you experience and practice dying every night as you go to bed!!

The difference between dying and sleeping is that you waken up in a different place when you die. We know, with all our heart and mind, that between Jesus dying on the Cross on the hill called Calvary and His Resurrection from His Garden Tomb, He certainly was not unconscious and inactive but incredibly involved. On His Resurrection He received a new body with which He ascended to heaven. So those who have died in the reality of God's salvation await their resurrection fully aware and wonderfully enjoying the environment of God's Paradise and experiencing the transforming reality of God's presence.

On that remarkable and unique Day when Jesus comes out of eternity into history again, He will bring with Him those who are awaiting their resurrection in Paradise first of all. They shall receive their new resurrection bodies first. Then those who have acknowledged Jesus as Lord and Saviour and are still alive on earth on that Day of His Returning will be gathered up with that great company of the followers of Jesus from Paradise in the biggest Meeting of Christians anywhere, ever – in the air because there is no other location big enough.

It will not be a time of secrecy and silence, for all of creation will be aware of what is happening – the clear, authoritative call of the glorified Messiah will be heard; the highest ranking of the heavenly messengers will join in; and the clarion announcement of God Himself will be sounded forth and those about whom you have been so anxious will appear in their new, resurrected bodies.

Only after that spectacular and overwhelming reality has happened will those redeemed by the perfect sacrifice of the Lord Jesus Christ on the Cross, and are still alive on earth, be transformed into their final glory and be gathered into the praising, exalting company of the redeemed by the Redeemer. From that Day onwards nothing will ever separate us from Jesus – the King of kings. So never be downhearted ever again – we shall be with Him, and with His from eternity as well as history, forever! Look forward not backward!!

∼CHAPTER 5 ∼

I so realise there is a persistent and dominant question which haunts every thinking, Christian's mind – although you know perfectly well there is no answer. When will all this incredible-end-times-drama occur? How wise of God to keep it a hidden and closely guarded secret – even Jesus did not know! You see, if we knew it was near our human frailty would panic. On the other hand if we knew it was distant our humanity would procrastinate.

However, one thing is sure so far as you are concerned – His Coming will be like the strategy of the burglar. His stock-in-trade is surprise, particularly when it is dark. Generally human nature has a strong and disastrous tendency to be lulled into a false sense of security – wanting tolerance rather than truth. Sentiment rather than Scripture dictates its reactions.

Be absolutely and definitely assured that there is neither encouragement nor comfort apart from Jesus, either in history or in eternity. Darkness, despair, and disintegration will assuredly come as unexpectedly as a woman giving birth to her child – unprepared and irresistible. However uncomfortable and unacceptable it is, there is no Plan B for those who refuse to accept the overwhelmingly generous offer of God's heart in His Son, Jesus. This is not a call to become religious but an eternal heart-cry to become real.

Thank God, dear friends, this does not apply to any of you. You will not be taken unawares and found desperately wanting. For you the dawn has come and the night has gone; the day has broken upon you and the darkness is forever banished from you. It is for this reason we are urging you to live in the flood-tide of the God-life, aware of the constant danger of spiritual apathy and indolence and the need constantly to take charge of the events and circumstances of your lives. Never be tempted to follow the beliefs and behaviour of others who are totally unaware of the reality of the situation.

Darkness is the environment of blissful ignorance and illusion and lack of self-control. However, you and I do not inhabit that dream-world of unreality so we behave in an entirely opposite way. Our lives are characterized by sobriety not intoxication – guarding and protecting our hearts with confidence in a God who is absolutely trustworthy and utterly reliable and trusting Him to provide the best, the most, and the highest for us (unearned and undeserved for sure!) and at the same time protecting our minds from negative thinking; debilitating despair; and godless hopelessness.

This God of ours does not have the searing punishment of His anger in mind for us, but rather the ultimate consequence of knowing freedom, forgiveness, and hope because of what the God-come-to-earth-Messiah accomplished for us, when He died on the Cross. He did what He did there on the hill of Calvary so that whether dead or alive we would know His infinitely transforming company and friendship forever and forever. These are the eternity-based, God-earthed, Christ-authenticated realities that you must share together, so that you will remain strong and resilient whatever your circumstances. My understanding, because of all that I have heard from Timothy, is that that is precisely how you are living together now.

In conclusion, we plead with you, dearest friends to heed and carry out the following instructions. We are writing them in this concise way so that they will be clear and cause no misunderstanding.

Give honour to those to whom honour is due – not so much because of who they are but because of the position they find themselves in as a result of God's calling on their lives. Their involvement with you is demanding and unbelievably difficult and they are always in danger of being misunderstood and misrepresented.

As fellow-believers they are required by God to have authority over you; lead you; and make God's vision to you become reality through you. Added to this they have the responsibility of making sure that the God-life you are living is acceptable to and approved by God. Have an attitude towards them that is respectful and readily responsive and always with warmth, intimacy and affirmation. This will enable them to fulfil their God-given task much more easily than if they are in a climate of criticism and constant conflict.

Make sure that your own relationships are free from rancour, suspicion, and criticism. We cannot stress strongly enough, dearest friends, that you must carry with great humility your responsibility for others who are part of the Christian family. For example, caution in the strongest possible terms those who stray carelessly from the place God has put them to fulfil the task God has on His agenda for them; be a source of encouragement to the faint-hearted who tend to give in too quickly and give up too easily; with tenacity hold on to those who are prone to stumble and fall; and keep going when you feel that it is all too much and a sense of frustration strips away your commitment.

Make sure that everyone understands that to respond with evil to evil is like the beast in the animal kingdom; to respond with good when good has been done is unmistakably human; but to respond with good when evil has been done to you is evidence that Jesus is at work by His Spirit. Be eager to encourage those among you to demonstrate this undeniable and unassailable Spirit of Jesus.

Never betray the hope of the Good News of God in His Son, Jesus, and your confidence in the fact that God is in control of every situation, by being downcast and miserable. Thank God that the door into the throne-room of the universe has been opened for you by Jesus and no one has the ability to close it. Right at the heart of everything I am writing to you is my encouragement to you to be grateful not FOR every situation but to be grateful IN every situation. You see, this is what the God-life is all about and our heavenly Father longs to see that both experienced by you and expressed through you.

Whatever you do never limit the power, the provision, and the presence of the Holy Spirit in you, enabling you to live the Jesus-life in down-to-earth, feet-on-the-ground reality. Pay particular attention to those who are listening to God's thoughts; heeding God's agenda; and feeling God's heart-beat as they share this in prophetic ministry.

Be careful, however, never to be gullible and misled either by well-meaning or selfishly-motivated charlatans. Place everything in the context of Christ's teaching, Scriptural revelation, and godly affirmation from those who are mature in God's things – so you will distinguish the good from the bad; the creative from the destructive; and the helpful from the harmful.

The deepest desire of my heart for you all is that God Himself, who treasures our well-being, will enable you to live a life that is pure and pleasurable to Him. May He guard and protect every part of your personality – the hidden as well as the seen – from stumbling and falling so that when His Son, the God-made-flesh-anointed-One, returns to this planet He will find you blameless and unashamed. The One who called you in the beginning will not rest nor leave one stone unturned until He has completed what He began, for that is His very nature.

On a personal note, dearest friends, do not forget us when you enter the presence of God through faith, but keep us constantly on your prayer-list.

On our behalf, please give our warmest love to our fellow-believers with an expression of our heart-felt affection.

Finally, I solemnly charge you, with the authority Jesus has invested in me, to make sure that no one is left out from hearing the contents of this letter.

May the sheer undeserved generosity and favour of our sovereign Saviour be your constant experience and blessing.

THE GOD-LIFE AND ITS HOPE

Paul's Second Letter to the

Thessalonians

Paul's Second Letter to the

THESSALONIANS

~

~ CHAPTER 1 ~

THIS IS A LETTER FROM THE three of us- Paul, Silas, and Timothy. Our hearts go out to you there in Thessalonica who believe in God, live for God, and walk with God as you gather with our Master, who came out of eternity into history to be our Saviour, at the very heart of your fellowship.

May you continue to know the unearned favour and undeserved generosity and the inexpressible well-being of our Heavenly Father and His Son, the Master and Messiah-Saviour of the world.

There are basically two things we wanted to bring to your attention which we mentioned in our first letter but feel we did not develop sufficiently. Both have to do with how to behave in the light of the reality of the return to earth of our Lord Jesus. First of all we so wanted you to know what you need to know about this definitive, cataclysmic event which will bring human history as we know it to a close and usher in the incredible reality of the perfect expression and experience of the Kingdom of God. The second thing we wanted to highlight is what your response should be now on earth to that glorious event, to which the whole of creation is moving. These are our reasons for writing this second letter so soon after our first letter to you.

It goes without saying, really, that we are profoundly grateful to God for you, our spiritual family in Thessalonica. The basis of our gratitude is not some shallow emotional spasm but is firmly rooted in feet-on-the-ground reality. We know that the teaching we gave in our first letter – about spiritual growth, God-inspired and God-initiated wholeness, and the need for maturity- has been heeded and implemented with the result that your utter and wholehearted dependence upon God and trust in Him goes from strength to strength and relationships among you are developing and deepening in a way that is clearly supernatural.

Please trust us when we say to you that we cannot hold our tongues about you wherever we go among God's people. We constantly and consistently speak of you as an example of never-give-up trust in God and never-let-go confidence in Him although you are in the thick of unfair-beyond-belief pressure and impossible-to-understand circumstances.

All that you are going through is proof positive that undoubtedly the person who lives a godly life will suffer. God never misled anyone and His Son, Jesus, never hid His scars in order to win a single disciple. Your suffering is a proof to me that you are recognised as being in the Kingdom of God. Be absolutely assured that God will always, without fail, do what is right. He will bring retribution to those who cause suffering to God's servants here and now, just as He will give rest and relief there and then to all of us who suffer as a result of what they do here and now.

I am writing to you about this in the light of what will happen when eternity will comprehensively invade history again. At that time heaven will be wide open so that everyone will see the consuming reality of the Master-Saviour as He returns to this planet accompanied by the enthralling, irresistible hosts of heaven in irrefutable justice and awesome judgment.

There are two categories of person who will end up in hell – separated eternally from God. First of all, those who, in spite of the evidence of the created world around them and the experience of the moral law within them, suppress what they see with their eyes about majesty and might and meaning and order and design and resist what they know in their soul about right and wrong. They make no response either to creation or conscience and reject God who wanted to get to know them outside through creation and inside through conscience.

Secondly, there is another group that heard the Good News of God's rescue plan for mankind in His Son, Jesus, but made no personal response to it. The question God consistently and insistently asks is not have you heard the Good News but rather what have you done with it in grateful response. This is a supremely terrifying and horrific thing that I am now writing to you.

When God's Court has settled your destiny there is no further opportunity for appeal. It is in this life that we decide where we are going to spend eternity. You may well hope for a second chance but there is none. Instead, a great gulf is fixed forever and God's grace and goodness is no longer available. The image in which God originally created mankind ceases to reflect anything of the goodness of the One whose image you originally bore. The life-transforming, regal splendour of God is available no more.

Be assured that when Jesus returns to this planet the fullness and splendour of His magnificence and majesty will be demonstrated in the true nature of His rescuing love and abundant life, made real in the lives of those of us who have trusted Him, and we will be left gasping with astonished wonder as we really appreciate what He has done for us. Oh, dear Thessalonians, you will be in this company of those rescued and given eternal hope in God because you saw reality in us and responded to the truth given through us.

I so realise this is heavy stuff I am writing and a lot for you to take in but it is because of these huge issues that we are writing to you again and affirm once more that you certainly are on our prayer-list. It is one thing to desire goodness but quite another thing to be good. It is only God alone who can accomplish that completely and comprehensively in every situation in anyone. On this basis alone we are trusting that our God will look upon you with favour as you demonstrate the reality of the God-life in you, engaging in what will bring pleasure to His heart.

Our dominating and driving concern is that the comprehensive reality and indescribable radiance of our Master and Rescuer's true nature may be resident in you and that your life may be completely hidden in Him as a result of the undeserved favour and unearned generosity of our always-is God and His Son, the Master-Sent-from-Heaven-by-God-Rescuer. On this basis alone you will be able to say, "I have finished the work you gave me to do".

～ CHAPTER 2 ～

Be assured that Jesus is going to return in the future to this very planet visibly, recognisably, and unmistakeably. On that Day – before His feet touch the ground – not only are the shining, shouting angels going to be with Him but we are going to be with Him too. I want you clearly to understand that not only those who have died trusting in Jesus but also those who are still alive on earth who are trusting in Jesus will be with Him – and all of us, dead and living, will be supernaturally and gloriously transformed to be like Him.

However, this strategic, history-defining event has been discredited by the fanatical; disbelieved by the cynical; and distorted by the demonic. In my first letter to you I dealt with your concern that those who had died before the Return of Jesus would not miss out, but in this letter I want you to know that those who are still alive on earth when He comes again will not miss out either.

I am pleading with you to realise that Jesus has not yet returned to earth. Do not be misled, beguiled, or confused by any – even when spiritually they appear to be in touch with God; rationally they draw attention to observable facts; or even when they claim, quite perversely, that we have said in some elusive correspondence which was clearly a forgery that He had already returned. The truth is that that Jesus has not yet returned out of heaven onto earth so there is no need to be restless, anxious, or filled with panic. Be absolutely and securely aware that this is a pernicious deception that is being promoted.

Before that Day dawns there will be widespread and obvious resistance to God and blatant and arrogant rejection of Him on a scale that has never been seen before, and an individual will emerge on the world stage who is the embodiment of godlessness. There is no need whatsoever to be alarmed, for God is still majestically in control of history and that man is destined to destruction.

So let us get the facts right, for we are neither dealing with allegory nor fiction here. This person who is coming will be a plausible incarnation of evil as Jesus was the powerful incarnation of God. His stock-in-trade will be removing God from the human scene; replacing God in the human heart; and rebelling against God by encouraging anarchy. Let me say again, however, that his destiny is destruction.

I have no doubt that as I write these things to you that I am jogging your memory, because we talked about them when we were together. You already know that the mystery of lawlessness is being retrained in the first instance by a principle – the principle of law and order which God has put at the heart of human society. But ultimate rebellion is also being restrained by a Person – the Person of the Holy Spirit who is THE powerful restraining influence against lawlessness in society. But in God's time these restraining realities and influences will be removed and chaos, lawlessness, violence, and raw anarchy will pour forth and the Man of Sin will be seen for who he is and what he is. But don't panic!! God is in control and His son, Jesus, will radically deal with him and utterly destroy him by His powerful word which not only is able to create life but also to cause death.

This self-proclaimed substitute for Christ will disintegrate in the presence of the magnificent, radiant, indescribable reality of the returning-to-this-planet Master and Rescuer, Jesus. Whatever happens do not be hoodwinked and beguiled by the activities of the Man of Sin. He will imitate the God-Man, Jesus, and fool multitudes and take them in by his bogus, supernatural performances. He will undoubtedly be widely styled as a wonder-boy by the media. Be careful, for he will offer peace which is not God's peace; prosperity which will never enrich anyone; and salvation which brings with it no hope or future security.

Every experience and expression of evil that you can think of will persuasively blind the eyes of those who are destined for hell. It is an incredible situation that there are countless numbers who do not welcome the truth but refuse it. They do not want to be rescued from their sin and hopelessness by coming under the lordship of Jesus Christ and so submitting to Him.

The fact is that they are seduced – by sin which is often so attractive because, fundamentally, they want their own way. The ultimate, terrifying thing is that God's judgment is quite straightforward and He says, "If that's the way you want it, then that's the way you can have it". To be absolutely blunt with you there are two men coming – one from Satan and the other from God. Every person will welcome one or the other. Be assured that our response now will determine our recognition then.

So much for the gloom and doom, but now I want to turn to another aspect of reality which is bright and glorious and full of hope. I want to share with you the wonderful reality of predestination and freewill. This is about what God does and how we respond; His part and our part. I know that this will be difficult for you to grasp completely because we are dealing here with life rather than logic; with experience rather than explanation.

Dear family of God at Thessalonica, it fills me with profound gratitude to God that from before the first dawning of the morning of time – in eternity – God took the initiative with you and chose you. It was God who set this process in motion. Indeed, the foundation of every Christian's faith is not his choice of God but God's choice of him. Notice that God chooses people by two means – the work of the Holy Spirit and the Word of Holy Scripture. Both of these are so clearly displayed in your lives. Wonder upon wonder God not only chose you but also called you.

The question is: What did He call you to? The answer is: To share His glory!! You see, God's calling upon us is not so much defined and described by what we do but rather by what we are – sharers of the Master-sent-from-God-Rescuer's very nature. How on earth does God accomplish this? He begins with the undeserved and unearned Good News that we brought to you from Him and ends with the fullness, the brightness, the splendour of His very own nature. In other words God connects you through the Gospel to His glory.

Oh dear, dear friends, never settle for less than God's best and never be content with less than God's highest for you. It is because of this magnificent reality, dear family of God at Thessalonica, that I am pleading with you not to budge one inch from the convictions upon which you now stand, and which you hold dear, which are based on the clear instructions and truth that we have shared with you, whether during the time we were with you or subsequently through our correspondence with you.

Please realise this is neither a call nor a command to try harder or to do more. This is all about our Master-sent-from-God-Rescuer and, indeed, our ever-loving, caring, intimate, embracing heavenly Father being allowed to do in our lives what They want to do – to perfect us to live righteous lives both in our conduct and in our conversations. The longing and yearning of God's heart is not only to prevent us from falling but also to present us faultless one day in His presence.

～ Chapter 3 ～

As I come to the end of this letter I want to ask you, dear family of God at Thessalonica, constantly to hold us before God in your prayers, that the transforming truth about our Master-Saviour may be widely heard and responded to in the same way that you responded to Him. Please pray for our protection from perverse and twisted people who are intent on discrediting our Message and destroying us. We have discovered opposition to our ministry and our calling in our Lord Jesus from the most unlikely people in the most unusual places.

However, God never fails and He will resource you and watch over you as you face attacks from the dominion of darkness. You already must know that you are called to be soldiers for God as well as to be His sons and His servants. God knows – and He wants you to know – that it is not only difficult to be a Christian but it is dangerous too. Be assured that we have no doubt at all that you are fulfilling the instructions we gave you when we were with you, and that you will continue to do so even though we are distant from you.

Divine sovereignty never eliminates human responsibility. God wants to lead you in two directions at the same time – loving Him and having compassion for people. So let me emphasize again the responsibilities you have – continue to have unshakeable confidence in the Good News we brought you; stand firm and hold on to the truth even when some would undermine your stability and beguile you into taking another way; continue to pray that God's work will grow; and finally bless God and benefit others.

I cannot stress too strongly – and so I am using the authority of our Mater-sent-from-God-Rescuer – shun every Christian who takes something out of society without putting anything back into it. There is a problem among you that needs to be addressed and confronted – laziness!! You will clearly remember that when we were with you we not only preached the Cross, the Resurrection, and the Return of Christ but we gave you biblical teaching on work. You saw how hard we worked when we were with you. We worked hard not only to supply our every-day, practical needs but also to demonstrate that working is not an inferior or sub-standard way of living. So we gave you not only instruction and guidelines but we lived out before you what we were teaching.

We were always eager to pay our way and never to take your hospitality for granted. It was for this reason that though our lives were more than fully occupied we still worked during the daylight hours and into the night while others were resting. You – as well as ourselves – may well have come to the conclusion that you had a responsibility to care for us and look after us. However, you must have realised that we did not accept anything from you, not because of ingratitude or pride, but so that we could model something important in your community. So, while we were with you we gave this clear instruction and directive to be strictly obeyed: 'Laziness must not be encouraged or tolerated and indolence must never be recompensed or rewarded.'

In view of all of this it distresses us that some among you are clearly ignoring what we so clearly taught and disregarding how we so consistently lived. The great danger of indolence is that, lacking a focus for their own lives, the indolent meddle and interfere with the lives of others. It is with all the authority of someone who has been encountered and confronted by the risen Jesus; submitted and surrendered to the reigning Master; and recognising and responding to that divine, anointed One sent from God, that I challenge and call anyone among you in this category to get a realistic grip of their lives and behave in a responsible way. So, family of

God there in Thessalonica, never weary in well-doing but constantly bring pleasure to God's heart.

To be very practical, clearly identify any who disregard our guidance and dismiss our teaching. Be pro-active and firm towards people like that and consciously withdraw fellowship from them and blacklist them so that they and others might know what is going on. It is not that they oppose or attack the Kingdom of God, but they are dangerous to it and discredit themselves. Let them be in no doubt that their behaviour is unacceptable and their attitude needs to change.

All that remains for me to say is that I want you to know God's well-being whatever your circumstances. May all of you, without exception, know His presence on your journey.

Although this letter comes from all three of us I want you to know that it is Paul who is actually writing it. You will know my handwriting and so be able to feel secure in its authenticity.

May the unearned favour and undeserved generosity of our Mater-sent-from-God-Saviour be the living experience of every one of you.

THE GOD-LIFE AND ITS PASTORAL CARE

Paul's First Letter to

Timothy

Paul's First Letter to

TIMOTHY

∼ CHAPTER 1 ∼

DEAR TIMOTHY, THIS IS PAUL writing to you – the one amazingly sent out as an ambassador of God's eternally Anointed One, Jesus, by the specific, divine appointment of God Himself, to be our Rescuer and Deliverer. And that same eternally Anointed One, Jesus, is our stability in the midst of cultural chaos and our security whatever the future might hold for us.

I am sending this letter to you as one of a new generation of young men who are clearly committed to all that I have lived for, because God has so powerfully revealed to me that it is true.

Oh, Timothy, may you go on experiencing the sheer, unearned and undeserved generosity and favour of God, realising that God doesn't give us what we deserve. And that the longing of God, our heavenly Father, along with His Son, our heaven-sent, earth-visiting, life-releasing Master is for our limitless and unrestricted well-being.

You will remember how strongly I impressed upon you, when I set out for Macedonia, to remain where you are in Ephesus, so that you might exercise your very considerable authority as an apostolic delegate to demand that some (whom I will not name!), who are teaching as truth what is not truth, be quiet and stop getting themselves involved and immersed in romantic, fictitious, unfounded, and misleading tales and in biographies, ancestries, and life-stories which lead nowhere, because they have neither beginning nor end.

These people are driven by novelty; exalting the mind at the expense of the heart; getting embroiled in argument instead of action; motivated by arrogance rather than humility; and are guilty of dogmatism without the foundation of knowledge. They actively encourage division rather than harmony and so frustrate what is on God's agenda, which is based on faith, motivated by love, sourced by purity, supported by a clear conscience, and is free from hypocrisy.

Tragically and bewilderingly, some have been deceived and beguiled by these people and have become satisfied with vacuous conversations. Dangerously, they are not only infected themselves, but dare to impart this 'non-truth' to others in the form of distinguishing right from wrong while living in uncertainty themselves, yet giving the impression that they know what they are talking about and so they are right and secure.

Of course we value the law because of the framework it gives to life and the security it gives to living. At the same time we are aware that there are good people who live orderly, creative, and productive lives without the necessity of external restraints and fear of punishment.

However, there are also those who use their freedom for license to live their lives driven by their own ambitions and desires. They are unruly and insubordinate; defiant of God and flagrantly immoral; violating decency and profaning sacred things; devoid of respect and gratitude; untouched by a sense of shame; careless of the sanctity of human life; guilty of sexual infidelity; practicing obscenity; robbing fellow human beings of their freedom; and distorting the truth for personal advantage. And, frankly, anything else which is the opposite of the teaching which challenges us to goodness, reality, purity, healing, cleansing and wholeness, because it is based on the incredible Good news of forgiveness for past sins; power to live a God-pleasing life now; and a hope which is eternal and will never die.

This Good news is not a discovery made by human beings but is the revelation given by God Himself to us. Unbelievably, undeservedly, and inexplicably God put this Good News into my hands so that I could share it and others might live in the reality of it.

Timothy, I want you to know how profoundly grateful I am to our Lord Jesus Christ that though I realise I am not good enough; strong enough; pure enough; or wise enough to be His servant, He enabled me, and more than that trusted me to be His ambassador. My whole background should have denied any possibility of this ever being so. Without realising it, I thought I was honouring God when, in fact, I was taking His name in vain. I took every means available to me to destroy the people of His choice. In addition to all of that I inflicted pain on godly people for the sheer joy of inflicting it. That way of living still lingers remorsefully in my mind.

It was to a man like me that God withheld His hand and didn't give me what I deserved because the way I behaved was the result of a blinded mind and a deeply prejudiced heart. The sheer undeserved generosity and favour of God was lavishly heaped upon me as well as His trust in me and His unconditional love for me as revealed and released in His Son, our Lord Jesus Christ.

In the light of all of this, I want you to grasp, hold on to, and never forget what I want to say to you now because it will hold you tight when you feel most vulnerable and insecure. The magnificent reason why God, the Father, released His Son, Jesus, out of eternity into history was to rescue the lost, cleanse the dirty, give dignity to the undeserving, establish hope for the despairing, bring light into the darkness, and secure a future forever for frail, failing humanity. Believe me when I say that I am the one who benefitted most from this and, in reality, deserved it least of all.

You see, God had a plan in not giving me what I most deserved so that I might be a visual aid of the endless restraint of Jesus in dealing with people like me and so enabling me to enter into what God created me to experience and enjoy through my ears, rather than with my hands. No wonder my heart explodes with gratitude, worship, and praise to the only Supreme God who really is – the God who has no body because He is invisible; the God who has no birthdays because He is eternal; and the God who has no boundaries because He is omnipresent and omnipotent. It is on this God that my eyes are set; my focus is fixed; and my hope is built as long as life shall last and then forevermore. Oh, Timothy, may it ever be so!!

My dear young disciple and colleague in Christ, I want to affirm in writing the following directions, which God has already spoken into your life by the power of the Holy Spirit in years gone by, so that by responding to them, as you live out your life, you may confront the demanding and intrusive challenges which are before you. Never let go your conviction about the essential rightness of what you are doing and the ultimate triumph of God. Never allow your conscience to condemn you, Timothy.

What I am writing to you is so basically foundational and crucially fundamental that those who have ignored and disregarded these things have found their confidence in God disintegrate and ultimately be destroyed. Among people like that are two people that you know – Hymenaeus and Alexander. I feel so deeply about this that I have instigated the Jewish procedure of excommunication from the protection and covering of the Church, so that they may well be subjected to some painful visitation that will be a dire warning to them not to play fast and loose with the things of God.

207

~ CHAPTER 2 ~

Before I go any further, I cannot impress upon you too strongly that you need to bring every obvious, common need to God, realising that there are things only God can satisfy in the human condition. Be constantly aware that there are no boundaries to God's provision and power and the door into His presence is always open and no one can close it because Jesus has opened it.

Because of this there is never any need to complain and grumble. Instead, be eager to say thank-you to Him because of who He is and because of what He does. Refuse to restrict your praying for God is concerned for the rich and the poor, the strong and the weak, the competent and the helpless, the king and the commoner, the aristocrat and the peasant, the mentally alert and the feeble-minded.

Particularly – as you are praying – bear in mind the importance of praying for those appointed by the political process to have authority over you, even though they are hostile to you and patently bear no goodwill towards you. You see, in spite of their human pretentiousness and their desire often to dominate others by fear or by force, they do create and promote an atmosphere and climate of law and order, enabling us to live our lives pleasing God and honouring His desires.

That kind of atmosphere and ethos is not only attractive to us but brings pleasure to our salvation-concerned God, who wants everyone to be wholly and eternally reconciled to Himself. To achieve this we need to be constantly aware that there is only one Person who not only brought God to mankind but continually wants to bring men and women to God – and His name is the Anointed One, Jesus, who willingly and sacrificially took the punishment that we deserved for our sinfulness in order that we might be forgiven, cleansed, and set free.

You can't keep that reality hidden forever, even when there is hostile pressure to suppress the Good News of Jesus. I know that you know this but it constantly fills me with amazement and awe so that I have to repeat it again and again – God called and commissioned me to declare this message of the King from the throne room of the universe and I have the responsibility of helping non-Jews to understand the implication of these amazing things in the way that they live.

I want you to know that there are no restrictions or limitations on anyone, wherever they come from and whatever their rank or race, to have direct access to a holy God because of what Jesus has accomplished for them on the Cross of Calvary. Resentment, conflict, and quarrelling over this are gone forever.

It may seem trivial in this context in which I am writing, but I am aware of the local situation where you are called to lead the local church. I want to address it now by saying that appearance is not everything, yet it often belies something much deeper and more significant. Appropriateness and sensitivity to the local situation will always be appreciated and undoubtedly have its effect. It is not so much how a woman dresses that matters but what she is and how she lives will always be visible evidence of her godly character.

Our culture affirms very clearly the difference between men and women and I want to preserve that. In the beginning, God showed us that men and women are the same, yet different, for both men and women are like God but unlike each other. Genesis Chapter 1 teaches us that there is equality between the sexes while Genesis Chapter 2 teaches us that there is difference between the sexes. From the revelation of God in the Book of Genesis woman was created from man (not the other way around as you would have expected!).

It is equally true that woman was created after man (another reversal of the expected procedure!) with the social implications that go along with that. Added to all of this woman was the first to be spiritually beguiled. We will never begin to understand the implication of all of this unless we realise that from the beginning God had a prophetic purpose in creating men and women equal but different – to demonstrate the divine initiative through the male and the human response through the female.

Clearly women have a high calling in God – to give God the family to love that He is looking for – to demonstrate the invisible as if it were visible; expressing the nature of God's heart as they seek the best and the most for those around them and live differently in a broken world because He is making them whole.

~ CHAPTER 3 ~

Timothy, I want you to hear this second statement I am writing to you – the first statement I wanted you to hear I wrote about earlier in this letter, that Jesus, the Messiah, came into the world to rescue, redeem, and restore broken humanity. This second statement needs to be heard with the same clarity and understanding as that first statement because God is a God of order and not confusion.

To want to be a leader after God's own heart certainly has His seal of approval. Leadership is never about status, but always about function. God needs, and wants, some to be responsible for the leadership of others and both to be responsible to Jesus Christ. Because leadership is such a God-thing the bar is set high. The leader must be careful not to leave any loop-hole for criticism of His character. He must demonstrate the chastity, stability, and sanctity of the Christian home. He must make sure that his human nature is under control, be well-behaved, and have the door of his home and the welcome of his heart open to all.

He must be able to unpack God's Word to others in a meaningful and practical way. He mustn't be addicted to wine so that he becomes quarrelsome, irresponsible, and even violent. His strength and energy must always be under God's control making him tender and sensitive to the needs and feelings of others, not constantly being contentious and controversial and influenced by the seduction of money. It stands to reason that the way he runs his own family affairs and the way that he relates to his children and his children relate to him will be a powerful evidence of how fitted he is to lead and care for the family of God.

It is important that whatever his age he is mature in the Faith otherwise he may become too big for his boots and act in the same way and with the same attitude that caused the devil to be ejected from heaven. The way he lives his life must impress those who have no truck with Christianity and never darken the door of a church, otherwise their barbed criticism of the Church and Christians will be shown to be sadly true and the devil will be the winner.

In the very same way those who carry responsibility for the practical, personal, and charitable aspects of church life must be men of dignified character; the same in their hidden-life as they are in their outward-life. They must be careful about their alcohol intake, and never be guilty of earning their living in questionable ways. They, too, must have a firm grasp of what it really means to be a Christian without ever becoming hypocritical and inconsistent in their behaviour. They must practice what they preach. To make sure that all of this is true they must undergo a time of probation and when that is successfully done, they can then be released to serve the Church in practical, personal, and charitable ways.

The wives of these men, and the women who serve the Church in a similar capacity to these men, must also be well-thought-of and highly regarded. They must watch their tongue and be careful not to repeat slanderous gossip that ruins reputations. On the contrary they are to maintain their dignity and be relied upon to keep confidences entrusted to them.

Those called by God to this responsibility must affirm and demonstrate godly marriage, be good parents, and run their domestic affairs in an exemplary way. There are incredible rewards for those living and serving God in this way. They are honoured by those around them and know the security and favour of the Lord Jesus towards them.

211

Timothy, you will never know how much I long to be with you and sincerely hope that we can meet up soon. However, we both know that life can become very complicated and the very best, thought-through plans we make, often need to be changed. It is for this reason that I am now writing to you in this way. You need to have reliable guidance about how you, and others in leadership with you, are to behave, because the Church is the family of God and the ties that bind human hearts in the community of faith are strong, resilient, and real.

Every member of the church has heard, understood, and responded to the call of God to come together as His new Body on earth to declare His Word and to demonstrate His life. How else will people engage with reality unless they not only hear it declared but also see it demonstrated in the Church? How else will despair be turned to hope; error be turned to truth; darkness be turned to light; deception be turned clarity; death be turned to life, chaos be turned to order; and godlessness be turned to godliness? Our message is clear – a baby in a manger; a Man on a Cross; a body in a tomb; and a King on a throne. No wonder we sing:

> In human frame He came;
> The Spirit owned His Name.
> The angels saw His face;
> The nations heard of grace.
> So many lives now captured;
> Before He left enraptured.

∼ CHAPTER 4 ∼

Be assured, Timothy, that eternity has clearly spoken into history and that as this present age draws to its close, many will be distressed and destabilised because some who once upheld, defended, and trusted the

Good News of Jesus now undermine, trivialize and destroy it because they are seduced by alluring heresies and demonic darkness which distort the truth and masquerade as light.

Those who deceive them do not practice what they preach for all sense of right and wrong has been obliterated in the depths of their being. At first sight they appear to be so spiritual, but they have blindly lost sight of truth. They teach that only the spiritual is good and that all material, tangible, and physical things are altogether evil. Consequently everything relating to the body and everything in the world around us is evil.

The result is they teach that marriage is unacceptable to the really spiritual person and that many desirable and enjoyable foods are off-limits. Clearly this teaching is an insult to God because He created all things in perfection and wanted what He had created to be experienced and enjoyed by us all as we recognise the extravagant source of it all with gratitude.

Now that you know these things you have a responsibility, with a gentle, humble, and modest spirit, to advise and inform those around you in the family of God of this reality. This will enable you to fulfil the calling that Christ Jesus has given you in a way that will be such a blessing to all concerned. After all, you have had the enormous privilege of feeding on the revealed purposes of God rather than the ridiculous philosophies of the human mind. You have not only learned from God but you have lived for God and found His truth to be so satisfying and real.

In the light of this, have no truck with groundless fantasies and childish folk-lore. Always make the main thing the main thing and make sure that your life continues to be based on rock rather than sand, on fact rather than fiction, and on God rather than on man. Keeping physically fit is important, but always remember that you are much more than a physical body – you have a soul and a spirit. Make sure you take time and energy to nourish, strengthen, and feed your mind, your emotions, and your will as well as your spirit for you are not only a child of history but a citizen of eternity.

Here is the third great statement I am sharing with you, Timothy, and it will require your wholehearted, unreserved, and comprehensive grasp of it. It is demanding, intrusive, and all-embracing requiring all the energy and effort you can give it. Our whole horizon is filled and dominated (and so our whole life is driven!) by the fact that our God is not a theology, He is a reality; He is not a fantasy, He is a fact; He is not far from us, He is among us; He is not destructive, He is creative; He is not critical, He is compassionate; He is not concerned to punish, but He is committed to purity; He does not want to condemn us, but He does want to correct us; He is not dead, He is alive and has come to rescue and redeem all mankind and He becomes vibrantly and vitally alive for all who will trust Him. Living the God-life may not be easy but it was for this that we were born.

Take authority and communicate these things in a way that enables them to be understood and then lived. You and I belong to a different generation, but never let that be a drawback in your leadership and in your teaching.

Deliberately resist anyone who would despise and dismiss what you do and what you say because of your age. Silence every criticism by your conduct. Let your words be measured and clear; your living be consistent and upright; your relationships free from bitterness and resentment; and your trust in God and your loyalty to God always unequivocal and constant.

Maintain your standard of honour, honesty, self-control, chastity, and discipline far above the standards of the world. I am hoping to come to you soon, but until then make sure that people hear the powerful, unchangeable, and authoritative Word of God read over them by you. Constantly and consistently avoid confronting people with your opinions and faithfully and clearly make sure they are confronted by God's Word that comes out of eternity into history.

Make sure that those who leave your Church Services are able to understand what the Bible has to say to them, and what it really means to be a Christian. Timothy, your ability to lead people and help them to understand what God wants in their lives is, ultimately, not down to your background, your training, your sharpness of mind, or your natural ability to communicate but rather to the fact that God unveiled His purposes for you through a prophetic utterance which the elders weighed, considered, and identified as God's word particularly to you and subsequently laid their hands on you and released this God-given gift for you.

Well, there it is, a great deal for you to consider and reflect on. Don't allow what I have written to remain as thoughts and concepts but with enthusiasm and care clothe these things with your body; put shoes on their feet and clothes on their back so that everyone will see distinctive changes in your living and, unknown to you, a Christ-likeness which is unmistakeable.

Oh, Timothy, take great care how you live so that truth and right-living are not only right but are seen to be right by those around you. Be constantly aware how you behave and be fastidious and faithful in making sure that what you believe and teach is obviously from God. Keep on keeping on, my dear young friend, because, in doing so, one day you will receive the crown of glory, as will all those who have responded to your leadership and teaching.

∼ CHAPTER 5 ∼

In leadership you will constantly be required to deal with relationships, but that is the reality of the situation. All kinds of tensions can result depending on how you handle these. It is always a difficulty for someone from a younger generation to address issues with those who are from an older generation – especially if confrontation is required.

Here is my practical advice to you – when you know it is your duty to challenge an older man, do it with courtesy and discretion but, nevertheless, with clarity and courage. Have it in your mind that you are expressing your care and concern for someone who could be your father. In the same way when you have to get involved in a situation that needs to be challenged and corrected with an older woman do so with dignity and respect, always having it in your mind that she could be your mother.

With your own peer group never adopt a 'holier than thou' attitude or an 'I am better than you' stance, but go about your God-given responsibility with humility and patience, emphasizing the positive rather than the negative but always making sure that what you are saying is clearly understood and requires a response.

Be particularly careful and constantly on your guard when you are involved with a young woman. The dynamic, physical chemistry between the sexes is never far from the surface, and so you must be careful to control your thoughts and never act in an inappropriate way. Always be on the look-out to care for those women whose husbands have died. They struggle not only with a broken heart but also with a heartless and disinterested culture that can leave them destitute without even the basic necessities of life.

However, let me be clear on this matter, that a widow's family needs to recognise their responsibility, down to the second generation, especially if she and they belong to the household of faith. The Church must be careful not to intrude, unnecessarily, into family life and deny them the privilege of demonstrating gratitude to their parents and grandparents for all they have invested into their lives. God has set us in families and we must be careful not to ignore or ride rough-shod over the order He has created. When all is said and done we live to honour Him by observing and doing, as far as circumstances will allow us, what He intended.

Clearly, things don't always work out that way and a vulnerable, abandoned widow should always know that God has not turned a blind eye to her circumstances or a deaf ear to the deepest cries of her heart to Him. She can be sure that her needs will be met and her despair banished as she trusts God every step of the way. The widow, however, who disregards and despises God's promises and provision and lives, selfishly, to satisfy her own cravings and demands, with all the disruptiveness and distress that

that causes her family, is alive only because she is not yet dead – she is only breathing not living.

I realise that these are far-reaching and often complicated pastoral and personal issues that you might well want to side-step, but I urge you to remember that to do so will be to neglect your responsibility in leadership causing personal, social, and spiritual harm to those who are involved.

I cannot stress too highly the implication of what I am writing to you now, for those who ignore their God-given responsibilities towards those who are bound up in the bundle of life with them. They are on the same level with those who are apostate and must be regarded as infidels no matter how hard and cogently they argue to the contrary.

I would like you to be absolutely clear that the responsibility and care of widows by the Church is not a random and speculative thing. You are required to identify and have a written record of all those you positively and practically pastor. Here are some of the characteristics you must identify before you put them on the Widow's List.

A widow is to be mature in years and never younger than the age recognised by our society as elderly. Her marriage is to be remembered for its fidelity, purity, and constancy. The way she has lived her life, both outside as well as inside the church, will have given a good reputation to the church to which she belongs and has brought honour and credibility to the saving and keeping power of Jesus by the way she has raised her children to be courteous, respectful, and responsible; by demonstrating her compassion, care, and concern for the stranger who needed a roof over his head or a meal on the table; by doing the most menial task that needs to be done with humility and efficiency to bless those of the same Christian family to which she belongs; by giving practical assistance, affirmation, and encouragement to those who are being pursued by the political authorities because of their public witness to their faith in Jesus; and has, through the years, been intentionally committed to blessing God and benefitting people.

217

Younger widows are in a completely different category and you are not required to take the same responsibility for them as you are for older widows. You need to be aware that younger widows, in the first traumatic, desolating, and devastating heart-break of bereavement, can be so prone to making extravagant vows and ill-thought-out promises that they will never marry again, but will remain celibate so that they can serve Christ and His Church for the rest of their lives – and declare that intention to all and sundry.

But, then, as time passes and emotions settle, their God-given natural instincts of sexuality and their longing for the companionship at the depth they have known and experienced in their former marriage re-asserts itself and their public, unqualified declaration that Christ is now her Bridegroom is clearly set aside and she is perceived to be inconsistent, untrustworthy, and lacking in integrity. The result is that destructive dishonour and crushing criticism is brought down upon her.

There is the added potential danger that having been released from the disciplines of marriage, home, and family life she finds herself with time on her hands. So easily she can begin to occupy her time in drifting aimlessly from one social contact to another repeating information that should have remained private, breaking confidences that people have trusted her to keep, sharing what is true but is not the whole truth, spreading rumours that have little or no foundation in fact, and giving the impression of understanding, sympathy, and friendship when all the while she is nourishing her own image of self-importance.

Because of this I would encourage younger widows, when they have begun to come to terms with their new, single state, not to hesitate to marry again when that becomes a possibility. I would also encourage them to seal this new beginning by having children and entering again into family life with enthusiasm and diligence. This will certainly avoid the danger of being a tool in Satan's hands. To be frank, my experience is that for some it is already too late!

218

Every local church is faced with its own distinctive challenges and this issue has proved to be a challenge to your local church, Timothy, and is a source of conflict, misunderstanding, and confusion, endangering the witness and reputation of the whole Christian community. It is for that reason that I am writing so extensively to you about it. Within our culture women whose husbands have died, find themselves without any realistic or adequate means of supporting themselves and so become very vulnerable and exposed to the real and humiliating possibility of destitution.

My final word to you on this is that if any Christian woman has close relatives who are widows, she has a responsibility to make sure they are cared for out of her own pocket rather than assume that their Christian family will step in. This, of course, releases the church to demonstrate practical and personal care towards those who have no other means of support in the political, social, and economic climate in which we live.

On a completely different tack, I wanted to draw your attention to the strategic and essential position occupied by leadership in the Church – whether they are bishops, elders, or pastors (incidentally, these names are completely interchangeable and refer to different aspects of the same responsibility). They have the huge responsibility to govern the people of God well. Those who fulfil that task with commitment, vision, and energy should be properly honoured and, where appropriate, properly paid.

A local church will only go as far and rise as high as its leadership can take it. You show me a local church that is dysfunctional and I will show you a leadership that is dysfunctional. By the same token, you show me a local church that is effective, relevant, and fruitful and I will show you a leadership that is effective, relevant, and fruitful. The evidence is there for all to see.

This is especially true for those who occupy a core position and sit at the beating heart of a congregation, because of their God-given ability to exercise godly exhortation and have an anointing from the Holy Spirit to make the authoritative, powerful, and unalterable Word of God understandable and practical, to those who will not only hear but listen.

Be sure, secure, and confident in the assurance that rewards are part of Kingdom economics. You will remember, from your knowledge of Scripture, that even the farm animals are considered worthy of recompense for their hard work. You know that on a Jewish farm the sheaves of corn were laid on the threshing floor; then the oxen were driven, repeatedly, across them to thresh the corn; or a threshing-sledge was harnessed to the oxen and it was driven backwards and forwards across the sheaves to thresh the corn but the oxen were left un-muzzled to eat their fill because of the work they were doing. As you would know, this was to fulfil the Jewish Law recorded in Deuteronomy, Chapter 25, and verse 4.

You will, no doubt, remember that Jesus Himself clearly taught that work done often implies money given. The sentimental ethic that we are to toil without any thought of reward, save the knowledge that we are doing God's will has no foundation in biblical revelation.

In the light of all of this, be on your guard and take note of anyone who comes to you to complain, criticise, or condemn a church leader. Leaders are human, and make mistakes like the rest of us, but because of their public position they are prone to offend or displease someone or other.

On the other hand, if several people come to you expressing their deep concern over the same wrong behaviour or the same wrong attitude in a leader then you must take that seriously and investigate it properly. If you are convinced, after proper investigation, that there is something wrong you mustn't sweep it under the carpet and pretend it doesn't exist but with dignity, sensitivity and appropriateness you must bring it into the open and make it absolutely clear that within the Christian family such behaviour in unacceptable and will not be tolerated. A leader's behaviour must always be an example of what is right and also, where necessary, must be a warning against what is wrong.

Timothy, I cannot stress highly enough how important these instructions are that I am giving you. They have not been written for discussion but for implementation without fear or favour. I am so aware that I am writing under the scrutiny of God, our Saviour-Messiah, and in the sight of the hosts of heaven.

Because of your position you will be required to commission people for specific ministry and service; to release the anointing of the Holy Spirit in the Name of Jesus on others; and to minister healing, wholeness, and deliverance on still others by placing your hands on their heads. Be alert to the fact that this must never be an ill-considered, knee-jerk reaction to a situation that presents itself to you. Take care and pray before you act. You must always be your own man and never be swayed by the popular, politically correct but unbiblical and ungodly views and behaviour of others. Make sure that nothing ever spoils your joy of walking with God.

While I am writing to you, let me give you a bit of personal and practical advice. I know that you struggle with digestion problems, so be careful about drinking the water that is available there, for it is well known that it is frequently contaminated. You will find it helpful to drink wine when you can and so avoid the danger of infection to your gut.

One of the issues that has constantly bewildered and troubled many of us is the reality that bad people often seem to get off with their badness scot-free, whilst good people often seem to struggle with misfortune, heartache, and even tragedy. It is certainly true that some live in a way that is obviously ungodly, immoral, and downright evil and in this life reap a bitter harvest because of their behaviour while others manage to disguise and cover-up their wickedness with hypocrisy, pretence, and deception and seem to get away with it.

It is also true that some live their lives in a way that earns them the approval, admiration, and praise of those around them while others live their lives unheralded and unnoticed in an exemplary way with constant unselfishness, sensitive care, and practical compassion. Be absolutely assured that in all the confusion and seeming irrationality of the human situation God sees and knows what is really going on – both seen and unseen.

∾ CHAPTER 6 ∾

As I come towards the end of this letter I want to raise some very practical and basic principles for you not only to observe but also to teach. For example, we live our everyday lives under the political and social authority of the Roman Empire. Slavery is a fact of life for us – probably 60,000,000 in the Roman Empire are slaves.

The first principle for every Christian slave is that he or she must show due deference and courtesy to those who either own them or are responsible for them. However difficult this might be, in many cases it will help to ensure that the greatness and the glory of the God of our fathers, Jehovah, is neither dulled nor diminished, and the understanding, in pagan society, of what Christianity is about is neither confused nor feared, so that the cause of Christ is brought into disrepute.

Also there is a constant danger that when master and slave both belong to the household of faith the slave concludes that spiritual equality cancels out civil distinctiveness. This must never happen since it can, so easily and so quickly lead to carelessness, inefficiency, and poor working practice. The very reverse of this must be the case, the Christian slave, serving a Christian master, must commend his Christianity by being a more industrious, competent, and a better slave than all his fellow slaves because he is serving with a new spirit, free from external compulsions and domination and he is motivated by the driving conviction that by behaving in this way he is not only serving his master but also serving God.

Another feature of our culture is the unsupervised, non-accountable, travelling teacher who effectively and professionally communicates beliefs that blatantly contradict, and inevitably confuse, what our Lord Jesus so clearly and consistently taught throughout His earthly ministry, and disregards and distorts what the Church has come to recognise as the basic, essential, and unalterable foundations of the Christian Faith.

You will immediately recognise these people because they are motivated by personal popularity rather than godly piety; by unbridled pride rather than Christ-like humility; by unvarnished pretentiousness rather than gracious submission. As you listen to them you will quickly become aware that their grasp of truth and reality is cosmetic, vacuous, and shallow. Their whole approach is speculative and argumentative, criticising and condemning all who do not agree with them, rattling people's cages, using language that destroys character, casting doubt over the integrity of others, encouraging bitterness among those who are prone to be negative rather than positive and destructive rather than creative. Long ago the life-transforming, God-encountering, Spirt-anointed truth has been stolen from them, and they ply their trade under the guise of godliness in order to make money and build a career for themselves.

And now on a completely different subject – money! It goes without saying that we need money to live in an honourable and responsible way. As we have already noticed, Jesus taught that the labourer is worthy of his hire. However, money can so easily and so quickly create a mirage of security and become a very persuasive deception of satisfaction and fulfilment.

To discover peace with God through the sacrifice of His Son, on our behalf, on the Cross of Calvary and experience power from God through the limitless resources of His Spirit is to become aware of who I am, why I am here, and where I am going. Nothing, at any time or anywhere, can compare with that reality.

The span of each of our lives is short and so we must live for the things that never fade or die refusing to become slaves to things that do not last but deteriorate as our days on earth go by. In nakedness we were born and as life goes on we soon become aware that there are no pockets in a shroud. How privileged we are when we have a roof over our heads; clothes on our backs; shoes on our feet; and enough money to put bread on our table. After all, you can only eat one breakfast!

Poverty is not a virtue, but money is severely limited in what it can accomplish – it will buy you a bed, but not sleep; food, but not an appetite; a house, but not a home; medicine, but not health; luxuries, but not culture; religion, but not salvation; a good life, but not eternal life. How foolish we are to fall for the delusion that this world in which we now live is everything; that some day, if we get enough money, we will be absolutely content; that our relationships will always be enriched through wealth; and wealth will make other people, and us, better people.

Money, like sex and politics, is neutral and so it depends on what you do with it whether it blesses others or curses you. Those who have pursued money as their goal in life and their god to be honoured have often reaped a bitter and poisonous harvest and have wandered in roads that are shameful and sad. Saddest of all are those who, in their pursuit of wealth, have dispensed with God and now live without any invisible means of support.

Oh, my dear Timothy, never lose sight of the fact that you are God's man – created, cleansed, called, and commissioned by God. Have no truck with these things and people that I have warned you against. Instead, with intentional commitment constantly give to those around you what is rightfully theirs and to God what is rightfully His. Live your life clothed with a reverence that stems from the fact that you realise that God is always with you.

Be trustworthy, loyal, and faithful so that those around you know they can depend on you. Refuse to desire and demonstrate to others anything other than the highest, the most, the greatest and the best for them. Whatever life throws at you, never let it get you down, but regard it as a challenge rather than a threat. Above everything else walk tall, treating others well, and never forgetting what God has made you. Face up to the challenges of life with courtesy, confidence, and courage.

When you were baptized you declared openly and publicly what you had discovered personally and privately, that the life of God had been birthed within you. Never go back on that life-transforming reality. In your head and in your heart take your stand alongside our Messiah Saviour, when He illegally stood before the Roman Governor, Pontius Pilate, and identified who He really was. Never deny who you really are in God however severe the pressure and whatever the consequences might be.

Be constantly aware that human history is moving towards a dramatic and dynamic climax when our Lord Jesus will powerfully and personally return to our planet to begin a new royal reign. Make sure that on that day – and no one knows when it will be – you are blameless and unashamed and so win His approval. Live with the constant conviction and assurance that God is on the throne of the universe in absolute and perfect control. No sovereign; no monarch; no dignitary of any description can compare with Him. He has no beginning and no ending. Human eyes cannot bear the sight of His radiant, dazzling holiness for He is the embodiment of purity as well as power. All you can do, Timothy, as you recognise and recall this, is fall on your face before Him in surrender, submission, and life-releasing worship. So may it really be!

Take authority and have clear input into the lives of those who, by any standard, must be considered to be wealthy. Neither commend them nor condemn then for their wealth but be aware that often a super-abundance of this world's goods can alter a person's character and make them feel superior to those around them in the Christian family. This must never be so; and when you see it in the church you must be bold, as a leader, and say so to those who are demonstrating that kind of attitude.

There is something else that you need to be aware of: those who have much more money than they need can so quickly and so easily begin to base their security in their bank balance. Both history and reality join together to teach us that while a rags to riches story intrigues and attracts us, a riches to rags story can often lurk menacingly in the background. You have a responsibility to draw the attention of those who are living this way to the folly and the delusion of it.

In this world our only foundation for stability and security is God, for He alone knows our need, not only in the present but also in the future and lavishly provides for us so that life is not bleak and austere but resplendent; not poverty-stricken, but super-abundant; not restrictive, but expansive; not limited, but boundless; not burdensome, but liberating; and not brow-furrowing, but heart-warming.

In the light of all of this, use your leadership authority to instruct them to bring help and comfort to others; to be unrestricted in seeing what needs to be done and doing it; and to be open-hearted as well as open-handed in releasing his plenty into others' poverty. Draw their attention to the clear teaching of Jesus that what we keep we lose and a generous heart and a caring hand towards God and towards others has eternal consequences that can never be adequately measured in this life.

Make sure that nothing spoils, dilutes, or diminishes the treasures of the Kingdom that have been deposited so confidently within you, so that generations to come might benefit and be blessed by what you have been given. Make sure that you are not influenced by an arrogant intellectualism that dismisses and discards the unchanging simplicity of the Good News that alone brings hope, reality, and freedom to us.

Be aware of false human knowledge that elevates man rather than reveals God and is characterized by theological argument and controversy rather than grasping the fact that God has taken the initiative and spoken unequivocally in and through His Son, Jesus. Our world is littered by many causalities from human cleverness who have lost their hope, joy, and sense of destiny.

May the undeserved and unearned generosity and favour of God be your constant experience.

226

About the Author

J IM GRAHAM WAS BORN, raised and educated in Lanarkshire in the West of Scotland. He was born into a very active Christian home and as a teenage boy made his own, personal commitment to Jesus Christ. With all the arrogance of youth he went up to Glasgow University to study for a Master's Degree in Social History and Philosophy, with a view to going into politics to 'change the System'!

Quite unexpectedly, one Sunday evening in church, God called him to be a Pastor. That was enormously challenging since the Church was riven by liberal theology on the one hand and a hard evangelical legalism on the other. After a huge personal struggle he responded to the call and decided to study for a Bachelor's Degree in Theology at Trinity College, Glasgow.

He was ordained as a Baptist Pastor in Dumbarton in 1956 and led the church there for four years. In 1960 he moved to pastor Viewfield Baptist Church in Dunfermline until 1968, when he moved to Gold Hill Baptist Church in Buckinghamshire. He led Gold Hill for 27 years and was then invited by both his successors to remain on the Staff team of the church.

Jim was deeply influenced by the East Africa Revival and by charismatic renewal which was sweeping across the country. During this time he was baptised in the Holy Spirit and began to apply the biblical principles of the Person and ministry of the Holy Spirit into church life. This opened up a wider ministry with Scottish Church's Renewal,

Anglican Renewal Ministries, and eventually as a Trustee of the Fountain Trust in London.

He became Chairman of the Eastern Region of the Overseas Missionary Fellowship and served as President of British Youth for Christ for ten years. During these years he travelled to South Korea and ministered with All Nations Worship and Praise Ministries throughout Asia for seventeen years.

Back at home he was able to express his passion for biblical truth and authority through Christian Festivals such as Keswick and Spring Harvest. During the last 25 years he has been deeply involved in Ellel Ministries and has had the privilege and freedom to teach what was really on his heart, confronted by a compromised Church and broken lives.

Jim was married to Anne for 55 years until she died in 2012. They have four children – Leslie, David, John and Andrew. What a partnership that was!

Sovereign World Ltd

For details of new titles
and information about all Sovereign World's books,
please go to:
www.sovereignworld.com

or write to the company at the headquarters address:

Sovereign World Ltd.,
P.O.Box 784,
Ellel,
Lancaster,
LA1 9DA
United Kingdom

Or send us an email to:
info@sovereignworld.com

*Most books are also available in e-book format
and can be purchased online.*

Would You Join With Us To Bless the Nations?

At the Sovereign World Trust, our mandate and passion is to send books, like the one you've just read, to *faithful leaders who can equip others* (2 Tim 2:2).

The 'Good News' is that in all of the poorest nations we reach, the Kingdom of God is growing in an accelerated way but, to further this Great Commission work, the Pastors and Leaders in these countries need good teaching resources in order to provide sound Biblical doctrine to their flock, their future generations and especially new converts.

If you could donate a copy of this or other titles from Sovereign World Ltd, you will be helping to supply much-needed resources to Pastors and Leaders in many countries.

Contact us for more information on (+44)(0)1732 851150 or visit our website www.sovereignworldtrust.org.uk

> *"I have all it takes to further my studies. Sovereign is making it all possible for me"*
>
> Rev. Akfred Keyas – Kenya

> *"My ministry is rising up gradually since I have been teaching people from these books"*
>
> Pastor John Obaseki – Nigeria